The Art of the Rhythmic Choir

The Rhythmic Choir of the Church of Christ, Hanover, N.H.

The Art of the Rhythmic Choir

Worship Through Symbolic Movement

by

MARGARET PALMER FISK

ILLUSTRATIONS BY

LOIS-LOUISE HINES

New York

HARPER & BROTHERS PUBLISHERS

THE ART OF THE RHYTHMIC CHOIR

This book is dedicated to
the members of the South Shore Community
Church, Chicago, Illinois, and the members
of the Church of Christ at Dartmouth College
in Hanover, New Hampshire, who have en-
couraged me in this creative art of religious
expression.

Know ye not that your body is the temple of the Holy Spirit? Glorify God in your body and in your spirit which are God's. I Corinthians 6:19, 20

I will therefore that men pray everywhere lifting up holy hands. I Timothy 2:8

I beseech you, therefore, by the mercies of God to present your bodies a living sacrifice, holy, acceptable to God, which is your spiritual service. Romans 12:1

Contents

Preface

Because all religious art comes through man's seeking to reveal his awareness of God, we respect its revelations through sacred music, painting, sculpture, poetry, drama, and symbolic movement. A Christian art knows no barriers of creed or dogma; it is neither exclusively Roman Catholic nor Protestant. The art of the rhythmic choir which uses symbolic movement is one of the many art mediums for religious interpretation.

This book has been written to acquaint people with one of the neglected arts of the church, which may help both to reveal spiritual truth to them and to deepen their own devotional living. It goes a step beyond introducing this art and its historic Christian background—it offers practical suggestions for those who care to pioneer in this creative expression.

The art of the rhythmic choir is not an art for its own sake, but, as true Christian art it humbly and joyously offers itself as a way to worship and glorify God. It does not connect itself with a cult or special group, but is an art that blends into the life of the local church.

In the gathering of information concerning the religious dances in Christianity, I am indebted to the research by G. R. S. Mead in *The Sacred Dance*, in The Quest Reprint Series, and by Renée Foatelli in *Les Danses Religieuses dans le Christianisme*.

M.P.F.

The Art of the Rhythmic Choir

CHAPTER I

Movements Express Spiritual Moods

Worship the Lord in the beauty of holiness,
Bow down before him, his glory proclaim;
With gold of obedience and incense of lowliness
Kneel and adore him—the Lord is his name.

Low at his feet lay thy burden of carefulness
High on his heart he will bear it for thee;
Comfort thy sorrows and answer thy prayerfulness
Guiding thy steps as may best for thee be.

INSTEAD of being sung from books by a conventional congregation, let us visualize this hymn as a worship drama
expressed through symbolic movement. In this way it will
take on new dimensions.

A choir of spiritually sensitive young people who have been
trained in the use of simple interpretive movements enter the
church from the rear. During the first line of the hymn they
walk slowly down the aisle with their eyes directed straight
ahead and upward as if drawn to "worship the Lord in the
beauty of holiness." As they feel their inadequacy they stoop
for a moment of humility and then rise from their knees to
express His glory with arms outstretched and faces uplifted.
They cup their hands as though bringing spiritual gifts as they

approach the worship center at the front of the church. There they kneel in complete consecration, their self-centered tensions released, their burdens laid down. Their relaxed hands touch the floor; their heads are bowed low. Out of their surrender comes upsurging power and confidence. With "praying hands" drawn upward by the assurance of God's concern they rise. Slowly their arms are widened and lowered to express serenity and trust. They turn to leave in the confidence that God will guide their steps.

Thus symbolic movement may reveal spiritual concerns and aspirations. It is an imaginative extension of intellectual conviction and spiritual insight. It may be rendered by an individual or by a group. This art is more than pantomime; it is closer in technique to modern choreography. Often, the group using this art is called a "rhythmic choir" or "motion choir." It creates rhythmic movements and design, to interpret religious ideas and moods.

This universal, basic language in which the whole self responds to religious motives is being used increasingly by those who seek spiritual enrichment in church, college, or other religious gatherings, and by both Protestants and Catholics. At the Roman Catholic School of Formation at Grailville, Ohio, there is a course in Rhythmic Interpretation. From Oberlin College comes this report: "The high point of the Christmas season was the vesper service given by the Orchesis Group and the A Cappella Choir. Finney Chapel was filled to capacity to see a service of worship in movement." From Sweet Briar College, Miss Gwen Eberhard writes, "The movement served with music to create a mood of reaching for spiritual communion with God, a feeling of the power of His presence, and the consequent humbleness before Him."

Young people welcome this type of expression in a chapel, on a hilltop, or amid a forest cathedral. The North American Youth Conference of 1948, the International Congregational Council of 1949, and similar gatherings have included interpretations by rhythmic choirs in their programs. "Camps Farthest Out"—which are for adults—devote an hour a day to group training in simple movements with religious significance. Their leader, Glenn Clark, has said: "Until we provide people with a technique for praying with their bodies as well as with their minds and souls, we are not going to draw the world singing and crowding into our churches." Symbolic movements help in everyday living by providing techniques for the release of tensions and the achievement of spiritual serenity and strength.

Both drama and symbolic motion were accepted as avenues for Christian worship during most of the life of the church, but were crowded out by an increasing intellectualism before and during the Protestant Reformation. More recently pageants and religious dramas have been restored to the church, and the door is opening for an increasing use of rhythmic movement.

As the door opens two things are needed. One is to understand the use of this art throughout the history of Christianity. The other is to know how this art may be started in local churches. So, in the following chapters there are practical

suggestions on technique and materials; descriptions of rhythmic interpretations of both historical and contemporary periods. The presentation of this art is primarily for both
Protestants and Roman Catholics, but is also for individuals
not connected with churches, and for those of other faiths, because spiritual truth and art have a universal quality in their
depth and breadth of meaning.

CHAPTER II

Deepen Your Religion Through This Re-creative Art

Man in a Rhythmic Universe

MANKIND lives in a universe which is permeated by rhythm and patterned movement. If we view the stars through the eyes of an astronomer, we see that the circling of planets in their courses is similar to a mysterious dance planned by an Infinite Creator. Origen, the poetic preacher of early Christendom (*c.* 225), refers to an early Christian hymn "of the stars dancing in heaven for the salvation of the Universe." St. Bonaventura (*c.* 1260) was aware of this parallel when he wrote that in the joys of Paradise there would be endless circling in rhythmic revolutions with the heavenly spheres as the redeemed sang ceaseless songs of praise. "Blessed in soothe is that dance (*chorea*) whose company is infinity, whose circling is eternity, whose song is bliss."[1] Not only the universe but the intimate life of each human being has a rhythmic pattern—even his breathing. The world around him throbs with rhythm—ocean waves, songs of birds, undulating movements of squirrels and dolphins, summer and winter, seedtime and harvest. It is only natural, therefore, that we are responsive to rhythm and patterns of movement and design

6

because all this is a part of our own life, our world, our universe.

"Rhythmic Movement with a Pattern of Expression"

Religious feeling has been expressed through rhythmic patterns throughout the ages. The Psalms summoned people to "praise the Lord with the dance" (Psalm 150). Early Christian leaders used the term "dance" to refer to many of the religious pageants and dramatic services of worship from the first centuries of the Christian church through the Renaissance.

Christians are accustomed to using for spiritual purposes a word which to many people may have a distorted connotation. Take the discipline, creative power, and sacrifice in the term "love." Christians know that "love" is surrounded with radiant and constructive meanings. But to many people "love" seems sentimentally weak, selfishly possessive, and especially sex-centered. Yet we hold to the term "love," as in First Corinthians 13, because neither "charity," "concern," nor "good will" adequately convey its fuller meaning. If the reader finds himself thinking of superficial or exhibitional movements when the word "dance" is used, he is urged to consider that this word has a long history of disciplined and consecrated use, and to accept a broad definition of dancing: *rhythmic movement with a pattern of expression.*

Value for the Individual

Before looking at the religious dance as an art form, let us see what value it may have for the individual. Paul wrote in his letter to the people of Corinth: "Know ye not that your body is the temple of the Holy Spirit? Glorify God therefore in your body and in your spirit, which are God's" (I Cor. 6:19, 20). The body can be trained to be an ally of the spirit, whether it is merely in learning how to release tensions or to create symbolic motions. Glenn Clark, in describing the spiritual value of the rhythms period at the "Camps Farthest Out," observed that "as one relaxed his body tensions, his mental tensions grew less." So these religious camps for adults have sought to provide people with ways of praying with their bodies as well as with their souls.

At the "Camps Farthest Out" at the Isles of Shoals Reverend Walter Fiscus had urged everyone to take part in the rhythms class, saying, "It's the way to find great release and a peace in your soul." A minister's wife who had intended to skip the class, joined the group out on the lawn and observed how the leader explained the symbolic interpretation of the hymn, "There's a Wideness in God's Mercy." "The music started and I followed the movements," she said. "Then a miracle started to happen to me. The cold hard shell of me which years of sermons, conferences, prayers, poems, and all the other phases of ordinary worship had left untouched, crumbled into dust. I looked at the vast blue sea as I stretched my arms to the side.

'There's a wideness in God's mercy
Like the wideness of the sea,'

I sang softly and prayerfully as I began to realize the vast infinity of God's love.

'And the heart of the Eternal
Is most wonderfully kind'—
The love of God flooded into my opened heart. Through the
most unexpected phase of the camp life, I found what I had
come to find: God."

There is a serious need for training in the creative technique
of the body-soul growth and health, for they are mutually
helpful. "To damage the body in the hope of helping the
soul is a persistently proved mistake," Gerald Heard reminds
us, "But to give the body no skilled discipline is as bad."[2]

An Episcopal Rector, William Norman Guthrie, felt the
need for training the body to express the spirit. Our bodies,
he said, must become active means of projecting deep, creative ideals, so that we may become "adequate vehicles—
translucent to that immanent Light of the Creative God."

Simple Body-Soul Techniques

The innate, creative impulse toward rhythmic expression
is either awake or dormant in each one of us. Whether we
have the opportunity or not to train ourselves to take part in
a religious dance, we do have many chances to develop simple
body-soul techniques: ways of relaxing, walking, and performing everyday activities, all connected with practicing the awareness of spiritual power. For instance, tension of hands is a
physical sign that we are carrying a self-centered burden instead of being open to God's care and guidance. The attempt
merely to "relax" is doomed to failure. But to say to ourselves,
"I know that the ever-present spirit of God will help me. I

am not alone. My life is open to His guidance," makes possible a release of tension that includes our minds and souls as well as our bodies. As we go to work or to shop we can practice walking with our heads up, our shoulders back, and our weight forward. Perhaps we may hum inwardly a song like, "I want Jesus to walk with me." When we hang clothes out to dry we can lift our heads as we raise our arms to place the clothes on the line, and in that moment, looking up into the deep blue sky, we can say, "Thank you, God." Possibilities for expressive, symbolic religious movements are all around us. Just as Brother Lawrence practiced the Presence of God in his kitchen, so we can practice this awareness of spiritual power and respond to it completely.

Body-soul training means that we practice the physical discipline simultaneously with spiritual awareness. We do not need to rush tensely getting things done so that we may then have a quiet time to meditate. It means that we cast our cares upon the Lord, releasing our tensions and thus gaining increased energy for our tasks. In whatever we do, even in our lowliest tasks, we can practice awareness and joy because of God's constant presence. Perhaps sometimes when you have found yourself humming the melody of a masterpiece like the "Hallelujah Chorus" you are conscious in your mind of the harmony of a full choir singing it. Even so these simple exercises of release and awareness which one can practice alone are like melodies, and the full harmony of a religious dance can be appreciated in the interpretations by a rhythmic choir.

Meaningful for Youth

Although the art form of symbolic movement has deep and valuable spiritual meaning for adults, it is with youth that the religious dance can most easily and naturally achieve aesthetic and psychological effects. It can help young people to realize religious experience in a new dimension. Young people from junior high to college age are the most creative and responsive in presenting a variety of religious dances.

The experience of the dedication of the whole person in religious symbolic action is so real to young people that it lessens the power of intellectual attacks upon religion to undermine convictions and faith. A stronger base for loyalty to the church is built through such consecrated participation than would be the result if that loyalty were dependent solely on intellectual discussion of belief or dogma. Instead of knowing "about prayer," they can say that they have "experienced worship."

The church comes to be, not a place of repression, but a sanctuary of beauty and inspiration in which youth can make a vital contribution. Here young people take part in an art involving the whole person, and also an art which uses great religious music and dignified robes of pageantry in the beauty of the sanctuary. In being integrated into such a service of worship, they feel that they "belong" to the church. Instead of sitting in the pew and looking on, they have a place of spiritual significance to fill. The adult worshipers recognize them as instruments of religious interpretation. So, the young people experience the deep fellowship that comes with belonging to a group that is earnestly seeking the highest.

Emotional Release Along High Avenues of Expression

Young people in a rhythmic choir realize that they are expressing contrition, devotion, aspiration, exaltation, and other religious feelings. This religious art brings emotional release along the highest avenues at a period when young people want to give themselves fully—body, mind, and soul.

The religious dance provides an emotional outlet for many young people. At a YWCA summer camp a twelve-year-old girl wandered into the woods, while the campers were singing vesper hymns. A wise counselor who had noticed her action and had caught a glimpse of her dancing in the woods, later asked her, "What were you thinking while the others sang?" "Oh, don't tell!" the girl begged, "but I was praying. Only who'd ever believe it? But I was! I just knew God would be listening and I thought, 'If I dance real well, maybe He'll see me and listen.' Because I just have to control my temper and dancing always helps me to do that. I feel good when I'm dancing. I don't feel mean at all then." Here is a groping child instinctively finding her mode of communion with God.

An art which releases emotions on the highest levels is particularly ideal for development in summer conference camps of Christian young people. Also, summer camps in general are starting to use this type of art in their outdoor Sunday vespers because of its appeal to the whole camp group, from the youngest to the oldest, regardless of the variety of faiths represented. The camper feels natural in portraying religious feeling in creative movement and finds deep satisfaction in doing so.

Actions Identified with Ideas Reach Youth

Ideas, when identified with actions, register deeply with youth. In adolescence, when there are many tensions and frustrations, the correlation of dance movements with great music, like that of Bach or Gounod, or with hymns like "There's a Wideness in God's Mercy," "Take My Life and Let It Be," and "Nobody Knows the Troubles I've Seen," releases tensions and fosters emotional stability. Similarly, when adolescents feel inadequate and resentful, and sense the "Everlasting No" which seems so overwhelming, religious dance techniques again come to their aid. These techniques, which include upreaching and outgoing movements, and the simple walk with the head up, tend to ease their resentments and tensions by changing the focus of their attention.

Actual changes occur. The timid, tightly repressed individual comes to enjoy wide, flowing movements, learns to relax the jaw and hands, and feels at home with the group. Gradually the change reaches into the depths and a new, secure, enthusiastic individual is released. Awkward, jerky adolescents learn to be a part of great religious music, let simple movements flow through them, and lose their self-centered fears. Slowly a new poise grows from within and they come to meet life with a new freedom of body, mind, and spirit.

Even as simple a matter as posture has psychological and spiritual implications. As Martha Graham says, "Posture is dynamic, not static. It is a self-portrait of being. It is psychological as well as physiological. There is only one law of posture I have been able to discover—the perpendicular line connecting heaven and earth."[3] Religious dance technique offers assistance to youth in formulating their heaven-earth philosophy, for it helps them to stand straight, to be radiant with grace. Delsarte had a theory that the straightening of the shoulders is basically expressive of response to the stimulating presence of another. In adolescence, while youth reformulates its religious faith, there are periods of loneliness because temporarily the Presence of God does not seem real. In religious dance training, the straightening of the shoulders is emphasized to symbolize the joyous assurance of the constant Presence of God. Of course, to straighten the shoulders induces other movements: the head lifts, the diaphragm rises, and the posture as a whole brings about a new dynamic power.

An inner assurance comes to a young person who learns to walk smoothly and without self-consciousness. The spiritual effect gained by watching young people walk with heads held high was obvious at the Vesper Service of the International Congregational Council, where sixty high school boys and girls walked down the two central aisles singing, "I want Jesus to walk with me." No hymn books were in their hands; the focus of their attention was high, and they walked in a spirit of complete consecration.

To bring to young people the highest in the arts of music, drama, and the dance will help to give them standards for evaluation. The low and vulgar forms of these arts will be unattractive to them if they have a chance to share in the finest forms.

A balance between individual responsibility and group co-operation grows out of participation in a rhythmic choir. Each one has a special place to fill and actions to perform to bring out the pattern and design of the religious interpretation. The practicing requires steady attendance and reliability. Group experience is one of the most valuable means of educating for growth of character and personality. "The religious dance offers valuable opportunities for social interaction where each may forget his self-consciousness and express his emotions in a beautiful and satisfying way. It becomes a happy experience."[4]

Whatever we enjoy, we progress in and learn more readily. Religious growth becomes arrested for many people because they do not have joyous avenues to spiritual understanding. Young people enjoy being in a rhythmic choir partly because they do not feel self-conscious or conspicuous; they belong to a group that is like an *a cappella* choir in its selflessness. This balance of individual importance and group effort is a door to further creative achievement and group interaction. Such an art experience is not a pastime for youth, but basic training for Christian citizenship.

Effective Even for the Observer

A church congregation appreciates the consecrated contributions that a rhythmic choir makes to worship. A spiritual incandescence seems to be generated from the combination of the beauty of the music, the beauty of young people absorbed in symbolic movement, and the beauty of the sanctuary. The art of the religious dance is not an abstraction from life, but a vital, instantaneous experience. So the observers in the congregation are drawn unconsciously into identifying themselves with the religious dancers. They find this a spiritual re-creation. As Margaret Applegarth wrote spontaneously after observing a rhythmic choir for the first time, she saw "true grace and self-forgetfulness" which had a re-creative effect on the worshipers "in lifting our spirits straight out of our bodies and then adjusting them back into us again as we too joined in longing for a similar grace and a similar reverence. I know that, as for myself, I felt a really overwhelming joy!"

The spiritual use of this universal language of rhythm is one of the rare religious arts which finds response in all who witness it, from the oldest to the youngest; the most spiritually sensitive to the seemingly insensitive; the most vigorous to those in need of health. Renée Foatelli [5] found attention and appreciation when she presented a Christmas program of rhythmic interpretation in a Paris prison. Her comment was, "The invasion of these souls by the spiritual through the rhythmic imagery of the dance was of value in prison." In mental hospitals patients are enthusiastic over rhythmic choir programs. At the Connecticut State Hospital a group of fifteen patients entered into a participation program of religious interpretations. At the St. Elizabeth Hospital in Washington, D.C., Miss Marian Chase is on the staff as dance therapist.

It is possible that dance therapy connected with the deep anchors of faith and trust can assist in a direct way in the healing of emotional problems. In the realm of physical healing, Ted Shawn testifies that his "Dance that Heals" has been a medium for better health and release of tensions for the observers. Lil Leandre who is experimenting in the field of health through dance has written, "I have found that in dancing spiritual themes a healing and cleansing takes place both for the performer and the audience." Surely the religious dance can assist in healing because of the emotional release and spiritual power that it provides.

As the congregation comes to understand this new art, it can have an important part in encouraging the development of rhythmic choirs. "As congregations have been trained to accept the return of music and drama into the church, so will they accept the dance. It will need a sympathetic congregation, informed on the values and meaning, not only of the art, but of the dance as a specific art which is the oldest in the world."[6]

The experience of religious insight that the congregation feels in the interpretations of a rhythmic choir has a spiritual reality like a new clear light that diffuses itself through the souls of each of the worshipers and draws them together into a mystic union.

Erika Thimey, who has pioneered in the field of the religious dance, has written: "Believing the body to be an instrument of the soul, I have sought to create a new form of worship through the art of the body in motion. It is my intention that this worship be not merely for the personal gratification of the performer, but that it serve mankind by bringing a sincere religious experience to the congregations that behold it."

For many people, it is a new experience to witness religion expressed through the dance. A common remark after a service with the rhythmic choir is: "Tears were in my eyes, just from the sheer beauty of the movements and the faces of the girls." When three thousand Congregational young people met in Bushnell Hall in Hartford, Connecticut, for a rally, the worship service began with a prayer interpretation by a rhythmic choir to the music of Bizet's *Agnus Dei*. Slowly the curtain lifted, revealing eleven girls kneeling in prayer. One of the rhythmic choir members described the breathless attention of the audience of young people: "As the curtain lifted, I was aware of an immense dark stillness, as if we were all on the edge of the Grand Canyon at midnight. It was hard to believe that there was anyone in that vast space." Such absorbed attention is a witness to the penetrating vitality of this art.

The rhythmic choir offers vicarious religious experience in symbolic movement—a service that draws people together in a unity of spiritual reverence, a universal religious consecration. But it asks of the congregation understanding and encouragement, so that it may progress in its high calling of disciplined commitment and spiritual revelation.

CHAPTER III

Encourage the Art of Symbolic Movement

To be able to encourage the art of symbolic movement requires more than personal enthusiasm. One needs to realize that the art is neither a mushroom-type of growth that is springing up in many places, nor an art that is being grafted onto Christianity in the twentieth century, but that it has been a natural expression of man from his earliest days, throughout all civilizations, cultures, and religions, and is essential for man today.

Historical Association of Religion with Rhythmic Expression

The close connection between religious feeling and rhythmic expression has been coeval with the history of man. Religion and the dance were at the beginning often the same activity —the form was the dance and the content was religion. The dance may well have been the first of the arts because it required no materials and so became an early and direct outlet for religious emotion. Among primitive peoples, religion is such a large part of their life and the dance is so bound up with it that the religious dance is of supreme importance. The sacred dance was regarded as indispensable at all the

crises of life and its performance was disciplined and extremel
serious. We see this in such survivals as the Rain Dance an
the Sun Dance performed by American Indians even in ou
own day.

At all times and with all peoples, religion has tended t
assume some form of dance as symbolic expression. Th
ancient civilizations of Egypt and India created intricat
religious dances to reveal astronomical designs, to celebrat
seasonal festivals, to lament at the time of death, to expres
worship in the temples, and to enact dance-dramas of thei
religious legends. In India the art became a distinct disciplin
of body, mind, and soul. Yoga has developed contemplativ
exercises for the attainment of higher states of consciousnes
and faculties. The traditional dances of India require tha
the dancer be "expert in emphasizing and relaxing the stres
of emotion"[1] so that they may be a means of overcomin
hurt and disappointment and reveal the "eternal dance" whicl
brings fulfillment of the Four Ends of Life according to
Brahmā. Shankar, Gopal, and Sujata have brought some o
these symbolic Hindu dances to the United States.

If we judge the Hebrew dances merely from references ir
the Old Testament, we find dancing mentioned seventeer
times, all of which are favorable. It was considered an integra
part of worship. As a general rule, the religious dances were
performed by the sexes separately. In Exodus 25, after the
passage of the Red Sea, Miriam, "took the timbrel in her hand
and all the women went out after her with timbrels and with
dances." And Miriam chanted to them "Sing to the Lord
for He is greatly exalted." David led a dancing procession of

Israelites before the Ark (II Samuel 6). Even to this day, during the annual pilgrimage to David's tomb in Jerusalem, there is music and dancing. W. O. E. Oesterly in *The Sacred Dance*[2] gives a complete analysis of ancient Hebrew dancing, describing the festival, wedding, and ecstatic dances.

Knowledge of Greek religious dances can be secured at libraries so we will not describe the variety of religious dances which they developed. They had a special beauty and spiritual quality because of the balance and harmony they revealed. The Greeks believed that the dance was the art which influenced the soul most, and that it provided the expression for that overflow of awareness for which man has no words. The great Greek dramas made use of "choral dances" as vital parts for the expression of mood or the revelation of special meaning.

Glancing over the religious dances of the Orient, middle Asia, Africa, the South Seas, South America, and North America (*re.* Indians) we realize traditional dances are still extant and a part of their cultures.

Whether we look into ancient civilizations or into present-day cultures we realize that the art of symbolic movement is a universal way for man to express his faith. In A *Dictionary of Religion and Ethics*,[3] Hutton Webster writes: "The dance is a universal human experience of powerful emotions, such as social joy or religious exultations."

That Christianity has had a tradition of religious dancing has not been generally known, so an historical survey of this field is presented in Chapter IX of this book.

The universal use of symbolic movement is obvious in some

of our present-day traditional Christian rituals. The communion service or Mass,[4] has a definite pattern and is entered into as a sacred mystery with prescribed movements, gestures, and responses. Clarence Dickinson,[5] former dean of Union School of Sacred Music, New York, has said: "The dance lingers in dim reminiscence in the processions and altar ceremonies of modern liturgical worship."

Symbolic Expression Is Essential Today

But the religious dance is more than a "dim reminiscence"; it has a contemporary religious validity of its own. A. E. Crawley believes that "the dance is suitable for the expression of the most solemn and serious of controlled emotions."[6] "As a manifestation of religious and ethical feeling, the dance may be remarkably effective, because of the complete personal commitment involved in this form of expression."[7] Here is an art that Vergilius Ferm feels has religious value.

"Primitive art cannot fully satisfy the people of the twentieth century. Yet, when we realize the important role that the expressive activities have played at every stage, we cannot fail to appreciate the need for them in our lives today. In no age can man live in his intellect alone. Too often the emotional life is pent up within a hard and unresponsive exterior that repels fellowship of feeling."[8] The Protestant Reformation brought about the evaluation of many of the arts as unimportant or sensual, but made preaching all-important. "Religion which has disdained the arts as sensuous," Von Ogden Vogt suggests, "has not therefore escaped sensationalism. It has developed the sensational preacher. The oratorical may be thrilling at the moment but less lasting than the rhythms set going by the finer arts. Our view of human nature and of bodily life is very different from that of the Reformation theology."⁹ We have a new opportunity to use the arts to link psychological knowledge with spiritual insight.

Just as modern medical science recognizes the psychosomatic unity of response in the patients, so the church is becoming aware of a body-soul unity of response among its worshipers. The intellectual emphasis has been necessary but too often it has deprived the ordinary man of direct religious experience. To achieve this, most people find the need of an intermediary art which gives tone, movement, and harmony to soul and body.

We know that Beethoven had the ability to compose some of his greatest music after he was completely deaf, because he knew the harmony he was creating without the necessity of hearing it. For the average composer it is essential to hear the musical composition as it is being written. If Beethoven had not had a chance in his youth to hear tonal harmony, it is somewhat doubtful if he would have been able to make his later musical contributions. The church has been emphasizing advanced intellectual-spiritual theory, to a large extent, with the result that many average people have not had the chance to grow spiritually because the intermediary of the arts has been neglected.

Complete religious experience is like the interrelation that exists between opposite magnetic poles. When the intellect

and the senses are balanced, then spiritual power and consecration rise up within the soul. The intellect needs to direct
and evaluate the emotions and these in turn act as stimulating
influences in decisions of purpose.

Religion does not need to center so much of its attention
on reforming people as on re-creating them. We fail in many
cases to drive home our moral teaching effectively, because
we do not reach the emotions through some aesthetic form
of worship. For the emotional life, wisely directed, moves the
will more effectively than the intellect alone. "If religious life
is unstirred by emotion, it is little likely to develop the zeal
necessary to overcome the world."[10] So the religion of this
age needs to encourage and call to its service gifted workers
in every field of human progress: not only the scholars, mor-
alists, and scientists, but artists in their various creative fields.
Art is not a pretty or entertaining medium of secondary
consequence; it is the magnetic pole opposite the intellect that
can make religion a power in every individual.

What place, then, has the art of symbolic movement in
modern worship? Is not a disciplined form of body-soul
technique one of the ways to lead the worshiper to a fuller
religious experience? Evelyn Underhill, in her book *Worship*,[11]
has written: "Man responds best to God by a rich and com-
plex action in which his whole nature is concerned. He is
framed for an existence which includes not only thought
and speech, but gesture and manual action; and when he
turns Godward, his act of worship will not be complete
unless all these forms of expression find a place in it. There-

fore those artistic creations, those musical sounds and rhythmic movements which so deeply satisfy the human need for expressive action, must all come in." Worship which has been centered in vocal prayer may use an art form that involves expression through a channel which does not use words alone. "Gesture is the direct agent of the soul, while language is analytic and successive."[12] Allen Knight Chalmers in his booklet, *Adventures in Prayer,* asks: "Does God pay attention only to the movements of the lips and not to movements of the hands and body?" Similarly Hugh Benson, a Roman Catholic priest, has written, "We have no more right to condemn the language of the hands and arms than the language of the tongue. We are furnished by our Creator with all these members." "The whole body is the tool and expression of the soul," writes Romano Guardini in his *Sacred Signs.*[13] "The soul does not merely dwell in the body as if it dwelt in a house but it lives and works in every member and every fibre. It speaks in every line, and form, and movement of the body." The Christian, through the ages, has used the term "body" in a most sacred way by calling the church "The Body of Christ." Surely we can accept the body-spirit mixture of Christianity and re-discover a religious art using a fusion of body, mind, and spirit.

Need to Develop Sacred Art Form of Symbolic Movement

The art form of the dance with its rhythmic movement and expression in symbolic designs offers a vehicle for pioneering in this creative field. William Norman Guthrie wrote in his booklet on *The Relation of the Religion to the Dance*: "The Dance as an art of soul expression through the body should be restored as one of the most potent means of salvation. What art can accomplish this re-conquest by the modern man? It is plainly the Expressive Dance."

What is meant by the "Expressive Dance" which can offer the modern technique for the Sacred Dance? It is the dance technique which started (*c*. 1900) with the revival of interest in the classical Greek dancing, used free and creative movements, and gradually developed into a new, disciplined choreographic art. This new dance technique demands genuineness of movement and inner motivating power as its center. It is not the classical ballet technique with its prescribed, stylized, periphery-conscious movements, but a creative art of vision and conviction co-ordinated with total-body movements. Curt Sachs, historian of the arts, suggests the depth and scope of this art: "The modern dance expresses the joys and sorrows, the fears and hopes of mankind today. And yet, not only mankind today, but of all men and of all races and in all ages. For that to which it gives living expression has been the secret longing of man from the beginning —the change of body into spirit, the merging with the infinite."[14]

There is a spiritual source in the modern dance that makes it appropriate for use in religious dance. "Because the materials are derived from reality, the integration of thought, feeling and action which is present in a dance has a direct relationship with life itself and the life of the creator, its source."[15]

Because the modern dance has this direct relationship with life and admits awareness of spiritual mystery, it is an art form that can be used to express religious insight and religious experience. If the technique of the modern dance is studied and then simplified to an almost austere spirituality the church has here an art form that is worth encouraging and developing.

Renée Foatelli,[16] who has created liturgical dances in France, urges the use of the dance in pageants which interpret the Mass. She writes, "I envision the beautiful order of rhythmical processions. If we could learn to interpret the liturgical texts, sacred chants and hymns, by choral speaking, mimes and dances, we should be able to direct the people in rejoicings more wholesome, pure and naïvely fresh than those to which they are accustomed today."

Children, young people or adults can be trained to assist in special worship services through symbolic movements based on the simplified technique of the modern dance. This art of rhythmic interpretation "is not new, but it is a deliberate attempt to develop strength, beauty and power in the imaginative and the creative life of the participants and the audiences. Its immediate warrant lies in the need of our times for a spiritual ministry to the aesthetic and emotional life of our people."[17] The need for spiritual expression is vital, the artistic medium for creative interpretation is here in the modern dance, and now Christian individuals and groups are beginning to develop this sacred art.

CHAPTER IV

Start a Rhythmic Choir in Your Church

Wisdom in Using the Term "Rhythmic Choir" or "Motion Choir"

How should one introduce the art of the rhythmic choir? It should not be "entered into lightly or unadvisedly but reverently and discreetly" and within the understanding of the church. Those who are acquainted with it as "the art of the religious dance" should not call it that. I use the word "dance" in this book because it has been possible to explain in advance to the reader its full definition: "to move in rhythm with a pattern of expression" and to present its historical Christian significance in Chapter IX, but the term "religious dance" seems incongruous and sensational to the average person either in or out of the church. We suggest the term "rhythmic choir" or "motion choir" as people are used to both singing and speaking choirs. A newspaper reporter, describing Erika Thimey's religious dance program, wrote: "The word 'dance' doesn't describe it. Her work might more aptly be described as 'the poetry of motion.'" At present the public's limited idea of "dance" would not describe this religious art and so dance reference would destroy the opportunity to develop this field.

In a closely related field the Methodists are encouraging youth to learn the folk dances of all nations. They are putting out an excellent series of albums of recorded folk dance music and corresponding booklets which contain the description of the steps and figures, but the title of this series is "World of Fun" and the folk dances are called "singing games." They are obviously cautious about calling them "dances." Enthusiasts for religious dancing should take care that congregations are introduced to this art in its simpler forms. "In most churches, a lack of understanding of what can be done, prejudice and a natural conservatism have so far largely prevented the development of rhythmic choirs to anything like their full possibilities."[1]

Leadership

The leadership of a rhythmic choir is the central problem in the development of religious dances. The leader should be spiritual, creative, and trained in technical matters.

The spiritual qualification is extremely important. The leader must be sensitive to the need for dignity and beauty in a church sanctuary. If a leader is chosen primarily because of technical ability he may not have the perspective to see this art as a handmaid of religious experience. He should understand the aim of the church and seek to render a spiritual ministry through the rhythmic choir which should sense his religious concern both in the practice periods and at the time of performance.

A special Christian discipline confronts the leader, or choreographic artist, of a rhythmic choir. "It is difficult to be an artist and very difficult to be a Christian," Jacques Maritain[2] explains, "and the whole difficulty is not merely the sum but the product of these two difficulties multiplied by one another, for it is a question of reconciling two absolutes." But he goes on to encourage the Christian artist: "If you want to produce Christian work, be a Christian, and try to make a work of beauty into which you have put your heart. . . . Do not make the absurd attempt to sever in yourself the artist and the Christian. They are one, if you really are a Christian, and if your art is not isolated from your soul by some aesthetic system. . . . And if the beauty of the work is Christian, it is because Christ is present in the soul of the artist by love." Just as Fra Angelico remarked: "to paint the things of Christ, the artist must live with Christ," so the leader and choreographer and also the members of the rhythmic choir must "live with Christ" if their work is to radiate Christian beauty and truth.

Creativity on the part of the leader is especially needed. He should enjoy experimenting with movements and designs. His enthusiasm should inspire the group to co-operate heartily in trying various interpretations, offering their suggestions and selecting the most fitting movements and designs. The religious dance cannot be reproduced satisfactorily from a written description; it should not follow a set system. Ruth St. Denis' advice to those who feel an intuitive urge to create religious dances is: "Don't be delayed in your progress by feeling that you must dance (an interpretation of) a Madonna, or a Hymn, just because someone else does—not at all." The sacred dance should be a creative offering of each religious dancer and each rhythmic choir.

Of course technical training is an essential requirement for good leadership. To find a person who has had some modern dance training is not difficult. Many colleges and universities and even large high schools have courses in the modern dance. There may be some recent college graduates who are connected with a church, who would accept an invitation to assist in a rhythmic choir project either in the religious education program of the church or in a Christmas pageant. College graduates who settle in a community often think that the church is not progressive. It would deepen their interest if their ingenuity and imagination could be brought into the portraying of religious experience.

Until there has been more training in the field of religious dancing, it might be wiser to have a co-operative leadership. This would mean that someone closely connected with the church and of inner Christian conviction could work with a person who has training in the modern dance technique, and together they could present religious numbers that would not be possible otherwise. For many people that is a very satisfactory arrangement.

Certainly there is a great need for technical training among church workers. Robert Storer urges that "Schools of Religious Education introduce courses in religious dancing in the department of religious drama so that church workers may be equipped with the necessary techniques to produce pageants with rhythmic choirs." The School of Religious Education at

Northfield, Massachusetts, and also The Northern New England School of Religious Education at Durham, New Hampshire, are introducing courses in "The Art of the Rhythmic Choir." Theological seminaries could have courses in symbolic movement in connection with their departments of religious drama or religious music. Rhythmic choir "workshops" sponsored by churches and theological seminaries are valuable in training leaders in some of the simpler techniques.

How are religious dances created? They grow out of a combination of good leadership, a responsive group, an encouraging church, and spiritual power. The religious choreographer should enjoy the creative work of spiritual interpretation. And the members of the rhythmic choir should be patient in working out new numbers, enthusiastic over the beautiful, and sincere in putting themselves completely into their religious interpretations. The leader and the group need the encouragement and the backing of the church. This means that the organist and singing choir should be willing to assist them in rehearsals and in special services. They need to feel that the minister and the congregation understand their aims and aspirations. In a practical sense, they need some financial backing for the purchase of costume materials. This support of the church is essential if the rhythmic choir is to have an opportunity to grow steadily and to present its interpretations as an integral part of religious experience. When the leader and the rhythmic choir work together with such encouragement, they find that their efforts to portray spiritual awareness and religious meaning have been reinforced by a mystical

element of creative power and glory. They find that they have been guided and blessed while they have been working to glorify God.

Techniques

Religious dances are so creative and spiritual that they cannot be written out like a script for a play, but there can be sharing of techniques, source materials, subjects, and music.

The art medium for the religious dance is the human body, disciplined and spiritually trained. William Norman Guthrie, who used rhythmic interpretation in some of his special vesper services, wrote: "We advocate bodily movement: noble, reverently solemn and full of holy grace." Nevertheless the body, as the accepted art medium is secondary to the spiritual purpose of religious dancing. In the realm of music an audience may become so absorbed in the beauty of the composition that the medium (or instrument upon which it is played) is incidental. So, in religious dancing, it is the "selfless oblation of the whole body to God" that is fundamental.

Although basic techniques will be suggested, this creative Christian art cannot be circumscribed, for it is an expression of the inner feeling of the soul. "It would be idle to try to discover a technique, a style, a system of rules or a method of work peculiar to Christian art," Jacques Maritain[3] writes. "An art germinating and developing amongst Christian men admits of infinite variety. But all such forms of art will bear a family likeness and all differ substantially from non-Christian forms of art, as the flora of the mountains differs from the flora of the plains." It is striking to notice the "family likeness" in Christian rhythmic interpretation whether it is of chants in the Roman Catholic School of Grailville in Loveland, Ohio, or of anthems in a New England Protestant church. And these "flora of the mountains" have a distinguishing characteristic: their supreme purpose of worship and spiritual union.

To improvise to religious music is one way to get acquainted with the art of religious dancing. It is valuable as an informal class experience whether with children or adults. Isadora Duncan, who enjoyed spontaneous dance creation, told her pupils to "listen to the music with your soul, feel an inner self awakening, feel that it is by its strength that your head is lifted, that your arms are raised, that you are walking toward the light."[4] When people have the chance to hear great music, whether they are alone or in a rhythmic class, and let themselves be open to creative impulse, an experience of release and radiance will often come to them. Isadora Duncan had such an experience when she was improvising to the music of *Parsifal* and became aware of a "spontaneous creation of movements of great spiritual force." Often it is out of periods when the dancer improvises that unique parts of choreographic works are evolved, just as a composer may find himself humming a melody and later build it into a symphony. However it should be considered as an imaginative, spontaneous expression of feeling and not the composition of a complete dance. Choreography includes not only recalled and adapted improvisations, but designs rising out of techniques and set in a disciplined pattern of progression.

The religious dance is based on the technique of the modern dance which in its turn is based on the use of the whole body to express both feeling and idea. Instead of centering the attention on the positions of the arms and legs as in the classical ballet, the central part of the body is the motion center. The dancer first is sensitive within and then projects designs with periphery movements as the following through of that inner awareness. Robert Horan[5] describes the importance of technique as a means to free and disciplined movement: "We are burdened everywhere with a conception of technique that muffles instead of clarifying the humanity and force of performance. Dancers work and know it as their constant necessity to perfect an instrument so that it may be free of restriction and capable of the widest and truest inflection in motion; free from dishonesty and uncertainty; alive, spontaneous and exact." Some people think of the modern dance as angular and grotesque. There are extreme cases where that is so, as in many of the other modern arts. But the modern dance actually offers infinite variety in lyric and dramatic movement, in circular and angular designs, and in emotional and intellectual realism and insight. Certain schools in the modern dance emphasize certain types of technique, but there is a continuous cross-sharing of ideas. So, for those interested in presenting religious dances, it would be valuable for them to take part in classes on modern dance technique and to attend modern dance programs.

In forming a basic technique for religious dancing, a rhythmic choir should be alert to guard against nonessential or exhibitional movements. Training in the use of symbolic expression should aim toward a combination of spontaneity and control. Although each rhythmic choir should be experimental in creating its own movements and designs, there are certain basic techniques that include walking, kneeling, the use of hands, focal attention, and movements of exaltation.

To walk smoothly, with chest and head up, face and hands relaxed, and weight forward is a basic discipline of the whole body and fundamental in many religious dances, especially in processionals. Such a walk reveals dignity, assurance, and peace. Related to this is the smooth run which is used in the Bach chorale "Jesu, Joy of Man's Desiring."[6]

To kneel is a universal, symbolic act in all religions and it

has a variety of meanings. It may express meditation, humility, contrition, sorrow, repentance, or the complete giving over of self. The corresponding variations in kneeling range from the high kneel of meditation with the head slightly bowed, to the lower body position depicting humility, contrition, and sorrow, to the restless agony of repentance, and down to the prostrate position.[7] It is well to control the kneeling in going down slowly with the back straight and vertical. The bowing of the head should follow, not precede, the bending of the knee. In rising from a kneeling position, one should feel the first muscular impulse start at the center of the lower back, then gradually cause the shoulders to straighten, and continue up the neck until the head is drawn up. Then with focal attention high, one is ready to rise from the knees vertically with arms projecting as the final outlet of the upward impulse.

There should be attention to simplicity in the use of the hands partly because it brings a unity to the movements of the group and partly because it is needed to express a disciplined selflessness that points beyond the person. Fingers should not curl in toward the dancer, but be extended and together like the spiritual hands of the worshipers in the "Coronation of the Virgin" by Fra Angelico.[8] This use of the extended fingers is also apparent in the modern dance. Robert Horan[9] in describing Martha Graham's technique, writes of: "the fingers extended without tension, very seldom curved sharply inward. The extension of the middle finger lengthens the hands as it moves through space, and does not

swing the movement back in upon itself." The aim of selflessness in the religious dance requires that the hand should not
"swing the movement back in upon itself," but project the
spiritual expression through and beyond itself.

Just as the fingers of a hand have a definite spiritual purpose, so the eyes have the function of centering religious aspiration on a height beyond the dancer. There must be no
wandering of the eyes, no indifference to the high calling, no
meaningless shift in attention, for such movements detract
from the total religious experience for the dancer and the
congregation. So, a rhythmic choir needs to be trained in focal
attention to bring unity to the group and to create a religious
mood. In worship or processional numbers, attention may be
centered on a cross that is placed higher than the group so
that it seems to draw them toward it. If there is no cross or
obvious focal point, as in many dance dramas, the group must
decide where its center of attention will be. A general guide,
when there is no specific focus, is to let the eyes look beyond
and a little above the tips of the fingers of the hand that is
carrying through the dominant expressive line of the body.

There is rarely a religious dance that does not have a high
moment, and so part of the basic training is to learn movements of exaltation. Delsarte has said: "What is constructive,
good, beautiful and true is in the direction of upward, outward and forward movement." The uplifting movement of
the body starts from the center of the body, proceeding into
a projected release of the chest, as the back arches, causing
the upward tilt of the head. Then as the extension of the arms

through to the finger tips is being reached, the dancer rises to the ball of the feet or onto the toes. To accentuate such a "lift" there may be preceding movements such as a wide swing from an opposite position or a turning of the body that starts low and spirals upward into a "lift." In worship numbers, there is rarely any actual elevation of the body off the floor as is possible in leaps, but an effect of elevation can be gained through "lifts" that involve the rising onto the toes for the moment. Another way to increase the total effect of elevation is to have a platform with several steps which the group may ascend at a climax of exaltation.

Music for Religious Dances

The religious dance is usually connected with music although occasionally it may be given to the accompaniment of the spoken word. To find a suitable musical setting, one may turn to music that is already written, or to a composer who will create choreographic music. The latter is ideal but more difficult to find. The dance has been limited because it has had to adapt its designs to music previously composed, but there is increasing interest in composing music for dances.[10] The creation of many of the great compositions of Bach, Handel, and Mozart were requested in order to provide the needed music for special occasions in the churches. Certainly today there can be encouragement for composers in our churches to use their talents for occasional services in which a rhythmic choir takes part. "The organist of a great city church should be capable of preparing fresh music of his own writing for services at Christmas, Lenten, Easter and other seasons in which some of the great themes and experiences of the spiritual life might be set forth with moving power by the combination of all the arts."[11]

If we turn to music that is available for religious interpretation, we should look for variation of mood and an obvious climax or high moment. It is wise to confer with others who know the field of religious music and to try some of their suggestions. Then the rhythmic choir and its leader should decide upon the musical selection they plan to interpret. Musical accompaniment is usually on the organ or the piano with choral singing. Strings and woodwinds are also effective. Symphonic music may seem to offer an imaginative and sweeping background, but usually it is too intricate or overwhelmingly climactic to balance the simple movements of a small rhythmic choir. Music should not be chosen that has specific connotations of a different mood. When a selection has been made, sometimes it is practical to have a pianist make a recording of the music so that it can be available for frequent listening. The selection must be thoroughly understood by the group for choreographic use and a recording can provide repeated playings without tiring the accompanist.

The following are suggestions of musical selections that can be easily interpreted by a rhythmic choir:[12]

Processional type: "Holy Art Thou" by Handel; "O Holy Night" by Adolphe Adam; "Sanctus" by Gounod; "Worship the Lord" by Monsell; "Psalm 150" by César Franck.

Slow numbers: "When I Survey the Wondrous Cross,"

Gregorian-Mason; "My Faith Looks Up to Thee" by Lowell Mason; "Ave Maria" by Schubert; "The Lord's Prayer" by Malotte (See Appendix III); "Now Let Every Tongue Adore Thee" by Bach; "Jesu, Joy of Man's Desiring" by Bach (See Appendix II); "Agnus Dei" by Bizet; "I Wonder as I Wander," Appalachian carol.

Music with more variation: "Cherubim Song" by Bortniansky; "Angels We Have Heard on High," carol; "Russian Easter Alleluia" by A. R. Gaul; "Gloria in Excelsis Deo" and "Alleluia" by Mozart; "We Will be Merry—Alleluia" by Praetorius-Marryott.

Music for dance-dramas (from which sections may be selected for interpretation): "Seven Last Words" by Theodore Dubois; "Ruth" by César Franck; "The Planets" by Gustav Holst; "In the Beginning" by Aaron Copland; "Jeremiah Symphony" by Leonard Bernstein; "Job" by Roberta Bitgood.

Music that has been found satisfactory for religious numbers by professional dancers in the field of ballet and modern dance might be used for interpretation by a rhythmic choir.[13]

For informal enjoyment of religious music in practice periods, there is a wealth of available musical accompaniment found in hymns, carols, and spirituals. Some of these are: "All Creatures of Our God and King"; "Rejoice, Ye Pure in Heart"; "There's a Wideness in God's Mercy"; "I Want Jesus to Walk With Me"; "Nobody Knows de Troubles I've Seen"; and "I Wonder as I Wander." Shaker dance songs that are full of joyous rhythm are found in Edward Andrews' *The Gift to Be Simple*.[14]

If great religious music is interpreted with reverence, there will be a real spiritual value to both the rhythmic choir and the congregation. Doris Humphrey has said, "I picked Bach for music because I think he has the greatest genius for the very qualities of variety held in unity, of the grandeur of the human spirit, of grace for fallen man. Now is the time to tell of the nobility that the human spirit is capable of, give dancers a chance to move harmoniously with each other, say that there is hope as long as places remain where unity prevails."

The Spoken Word as Dance Accompaniment

The rhythmic choir can use the spoken word as rhythmic accompaniment. Psalms (such as numbers 23, 27, 100, 149, 150) and I Corinthians 13 have been interpreted through symbolic designs and patterns. It may be wise to study various translations of the Biblical passages and select the words that provide the rhythm that is desired. This was done when the rhythmic choir in Hanover, New Hampshire, gave their interpretation of Psalm 27. The last part of Edna St. Vincent Millay's "Renascence" can be portrayed by a solo dancer. The rhythmic cadences of James Weldon Johnson's "Creation" have been used with choral dance accompaniment. Choric dramas in which both a speaking choir and a rhythmic choir interpret ideas and moods are: "World Without End," by Albert Johnson; "Unto Us the Living," by Harold G.

Sliker; and "The Coming of Christ," by John Masefield, with music by Gustav Holst.

Costumes

The design of the costumes should enhance the simplicity, grace, and dignity of the members of the rhythmic choir. The skirt should be fairly long with enough fullness to add grace to the movements of the dancer. The typical costume of the Hanover Rhythmic Choir has a fitted waist, flared skirt, and long sleeves that are either wide at the wrist or gathered.

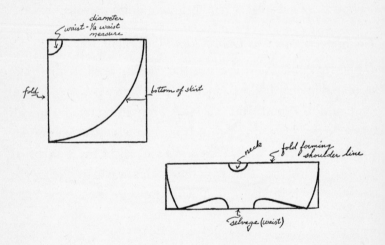

Sateen, unbleached muslin, and poplin are materials that are often used. White is a practical color for most worship numbers. A variety of overdrapes can be added to a white costume and in this way change the color effect and the design of the costume as a whole. One such variation can

be gained by simply taking a piece of colored material three yards long by eighteen inches wide, drape the center over the chest and catch the upper edges with a hook and eye at the back of the neck. Let the long trailing pieces hang at the back. The neckline at the front will have a wide, cowl-like appearance. Another effect may be gained by taking a piece of colored material that has some stiffness, five feet long and eighteen inches wide. Trim the corners of one end by rounding them into a semicircle, cut an opening for the head and neck twelve inches from that edge and let the rest of the material hang down the back. The front view will suggest the simplicity of a wide "bertha" collar and the back panel will add grace to the movement of the dancer. Blue and gold costumes as well as the conventional white ones, are beautiful in worship numbers. To have color in costumes is in the Renaissance tradition, for we see a variety of colors in the angels' robes in Fra Angelico's "Coronation of the Virgin" of the Museo de S. Marco, and also in his "Madonna Enthroned." Similarly, Benozzo Gozzoli painted colorful gowns for "The Choir of Angels Announcing the Birth of Christ to the Shepherds." Deep shades of blue, green, maroon, purple, or red add vividness to dramatic numbers.

If there is danger of splinters or dirt, the soft toe, white ballet slipper seems to fit in well with the total costume. Usually the members of a rhythmic choir dance barefooted. If any conventional soul is shocked at this, let him remember that Moses was told, "Put off thy shoes, for the place wherein thou standest is holy ground."

CHAPTER V

Let the Children Enjoy Creativity

O NE of the best places to introduce rhythmic interpretation of religious ideas is in church schools where
children may enjoy imaginative and active art expression.
Recently both the Northfield Conference on Religious Education and the Northern New England School of Religious
Education have offered courses on the art of the rhythmic
choir. "This is one of the most naturally expressive of all the
arts. Sunday schools are in a particularly favorable position
to use this mode of worship to give the children free, prayerful
and vigorous outlet for their naturally worshipful emotions."[1]
Rhythms periods are part of the three-hour church school
session at the Riverside Church in New York City. Boys and
girls from the preschool age through the sixth grade enjoy
this creative period under the leadership of two young men.

Very simple movements connected with hymn singing give
a child a release from the conventional procedure of sitting
still. Even more freedom is possible in vacation church schools
and weekday courses in religious education where there is
more time for special projects. In a vacation church school
Evelyn Broadbent (see pp. 185-186) accomplished a variety

of types of religious expression with children through this art with a prayer dance, dance-drama and a "dance of joyous fellowship" based on a folk dance. Dorothy Creed, teaching weekday religious education in Milton, Massachusetts, has used this art form in Christmas pageants.

Children enjoy combining action with singing. Beginners like to move in a circle holding hands like the traditional circling pattern of the early carols. A familiar song, "Praise Him, praise Him, all you little children," can be sung while circling. During the first "God is Love," the pattern can change by their stepping in toward the center as they lift their arms, then stepping back, lowering their arms during the repeated words. Again the design of circling can continue. A basic pattern with one change seems to offer enough design for the small child. If a circle pattern is used in the first part of a song like "Jesus wants me for a sunbeam," the variation can come when each child breaks from the circle to be an imaginary sunbeam during the singing of "a sunbeam, a sunbeam," returning to a circle form at the close of "I'll be a sunbeam for Him." Here the suggestion of self-dedication could be symbolized either by kneeling or reaching up. There are many new songbooks for the very small child that have songs to be interpreted. The two suggested here are chosen because they are known so widely.

Children of primary age enjoy imaginative rhythms that are possible in the song, "The seeds and flowers are sleeping sound 'till Easter time."[2] In this song the children can take the various parts representing flowers unfolding, raindrops, sunshine, butterflies, and birds. There is a chance for creative movement and at the same time a recurring refrain of joy in which they all join: "at happy Easter time."

In the hymn "Gracious Spirit, Dwell with Me" the following stanza can be interpreted in this way:

Silent Spirit, dwell with me	(seated or kneeling, hands together, head bowed)
I myself would silent be.	
Quiet as the growing blade	(peaked hands to symbolize either prayer or blades of grass)
Which through earth its way has made;	(hands slowly raised, with attention focused on finger tips)
Silently as morning light	(rise, head back, lift arms high)
Putting mists and chills to flight.	(widen out arms to sides and down, weight of body forward, face uplifted)

Here we have meditation, wonder at creativity, the lift in awareness, and released energy and inner peace at the end. "For the Beauty of the Earth" also lends itself to this type of symbolic worship.

"This is my Father's World" can be based around a circle pattern symbolic of the world. Imaginative movements may be suggested by individuals in the group. The leader should not have all the movements planned but should help the children to create their own designs. The children may try variations whenever the hymn is used at other times. If they are divided into groups, one section can work out its interpretation of one stanza, while other sections work on their special stanzas. When they come together the children will be absorbed in sharing their creations.

Members of the junior department who learn about St.

Francis enjoy working out rhythmic designs to his hymn "All Creatures of our God and King." During the first line they imagine that they are walking like St. Francis with little animals that came close to him. As they sing "Lift up your voice and with us sing" they raise their arms forward and up, thinking of St. Francis and his love of the birds. The "praise him" phrases and the "alleluias" seem to imply upward swings and wide turns. Just as the hymn seems to have been written for antiphonal and unison singing, so the group may be divided in order to provide antiphonal-like rhythmic patterns between the sections and then conclude with a unison climax. The devotional hymn "Worship the Lord in the Beauty of Holiness" (see p. 1) can be done beautifully by juniors for a church school worship service. To have them in choir gowns with white surplices gives an added dignity to the children personally and to the symbolic service they are presenting.

Children like to interpret ideas or stories with rhythmic patterns. This may be close to pantomime, but differs in that simple expressive motions are repeated in rhythmic variations and give the child a satisfying release. In a most simple form, a "thank you" prayer can be expressed, not with sentences alone, but by symbolic movement initiated by one of the children and imitated by the others. Such an action-prayer needs a period preceding it in which the children talk over that for which they are thankful. They share ideas about movements that will be the most expressive. Before the prayer portrayal starts, the leaders of each action-thought are chosen and know their order. If the pianist has ability to improvise music that fits the rhythmic motion, the group can be assisted immensely. Usually the rhythm will be in 3/4 or 4/4 time; so, if he has even these two choices in music selections, he could note, during the preliminary practice period, which rhythm each leader would need. Another means of accompaniment that is very successful is the use of percussions, especially a drum or gong. There may be children in the group who enjoy accompanying the action-leader's rhythmic patterns by using instruments of a "rhythm band."[3] A group of third grade children in Oberlin, Ohio, studying the story of creation in Genesis, made up their interpretation of it in symbolic movement to the accompaniment of a drum. Another means of accompaniment is the spoken word, either with one voice or with a speaking choir. In Hartford, Connecticut, a group of third grade children created a rhythmic interpretation to accompany the reading of James Weldon Johnson's "Creation." The symbolizing of God was portrayed by an older child who stood at the side, with back to the audience, watching the rhythmic group and using occasional slow creative movements. These strong, deliberate actions in the art interpretation suggested a parallel to Michelangelo's "Creation of Man" where the hand of God points toward the creation of Adam.

Children are absorbed when they take part in dramatic action. Parables can be interpreted through this art form. Keep in mind that time must be given for rhythmic pattern —that it is not to be pantomime alone. For instance, in the interpretation of the "Good Samaritan," let the beating of the man be done with special rhythm, and the victim have moments of reaction when he can writhe and toss with a rhythmic pattern. Here a good pianist can assist in mood projection. Each of the three men who come down the Jericho road should have as distinctive walks as Grandpapa or the hunters in *Peter and the Wolf*. The wounded man should writhe between each incident. As the good Samaritan brings the man to the innkeeper, here again the accompanist can assist with music that builds up the mood of accomplishment. With such a climax the children feel an impulse to identify themselves with the character and actions of the good Samaritan. Other parables that lend themselves to interpretation are "The Lost Sheep," "The Prodigal Son" and "The Wise and Foolish Virgins." Readings from the Biblical accounts between scenes or speaking choir presentations of the stories deepen the idea content. Scenes from the stories about Joseph, Daniel, and Ruth are natural material for this art form and help to make the actions of these personalities vivid and alive. Evelyn Broadbent has done creative work in connection with the study of the prophets. A religious educator in Iowa who was introduced to the use of rhythmic interpretations started to experiment with worship numbers and Biblical dance dramas. She wrote: "From now on I have a new teaching method. I had been wanting help in dramatizations of Bible stories; here I am getting it through the dance."

If children in the junior or intermediate departments are studying various religions, symbolic movement is a natural medium of expression. The children in the Oakdale Country

Day School in Philadelphia used this art in their study of the Roman Catholic, Protestant, Quaker, and Jewish faiths (p. 171). They spent time in figuring out the essential characteristics of each, the gentleness and peace of the nuns, the quiet simplicity of the Quakers, the vibrant intenseness of the Jews. Little was said about the characteristics of the Protestants! Perhaps their contribution might be concern in social service and in freedom. In St. Louis, Missouri, the children of four public schools presented "Man's Search for God" through a "sequence of dance and song." Secular schools are finding a rich response in using the art of the dance to express philosophic truth and spiritual beliefs. Surely our church schools can benefit by exploring this type of expression that involves the whole person—body, mind, and soul.

Religious education is more than training in worship experience and Biblical study. It also is concerned with the development of the personality of each child. Creative rhythms periods often reach the child who needs emotional release. Primary age children can work out their own repetitive rhythmic pattern to the music which expresses "No, I won't!" They enjoy giving vent to their negative emotions through music and action. Gay, humorous rhythms are as much a part of religious education as the worship numbers that have been described. It is surprising to see how many children have tensions in their bodies along with emotional insecurity. Simple rhythms involving walks and skips in which they learn to relax their muscles help them to be "at home" in their bodies and in this world. Ruth St. Denis states: "I see children growing straight and well-proportioned, swift and sure of movement, having dignity and grace, and wearing their bodies lightly and with power." Recently a ten-year-old who had had an opportunity for dance experience remarked, "I love to dance because it makes my mind and body strong and I am able to express my soul."[4]

Church schools can provide emotional release, experiences of joy, and body-soul training for children through this creative art, and thus help them to emotional and religious balance. It has been said that the happy child is the good child. If more of our efforts in religious education can center on bringing real experiences of happiness into the lives of the children, they will tend to make the right moral decisions and they will find that unconsciously they are open to the spiritual presence of God.

CHAPTER VI

Begin with Processionals, Pageants, and Worship Interpretations

Processionals

CHOIR processionals have already been referred to as reminiscent of dance designs in the traditional worship of the early Christian Church. In re-introducing this art of rhythmic expression, perhaps the accepted processional can offer a bridge to link the old with the new.

Each high season of the church year can have a processional of special symbolism whether it is presented at a regular worship service, a junior church service, or a vesper service. At Thanksgiving César Franck's "Psalm 150" can be both a choir processional and a dramatic presentation of harvest gifts. If the singing choir is in a loft at the back of the church or in stalls at the sides of a chancel, the attention can be centered on a motion choir patterned after the ancient Hebrew processions, with young people carrying gilded trumpets, harps, and timbrels, followed by a group carrying baskets of harvest gifts. As the last ones place their gifts at the altar, and as the singing choir reaches the four closing "alleluias," some of the processional group come to the center, turn and reach up in grateful joy and adoration. A candlelight processional at Christmas and a palm processional on Palm Sunday are described in connection with Christmas and Lenten pageants in the following pages.

Robert Storer (see p. 180) has created a number of processionals for his church. A basic pattern of his that can be adapted for such special services as Easter or Children's Sunday is outlined in Appendix I of this book. By dividing his processional choir into two groups he has worked out a procedure of dignified beauty and symbolic design that both children and young people enjoy.

As a general rule most people like the conventional choir processional for the usual church service. These suggestions merely offer occasional variations for special Sundays and ways to introduce the value of symbolic movement within the framework of a traditional part of a worship service.

Pageants
CHRISTMAS

Christmas pageants, because they are now an accepted art form, offer one of the most natural places to introduce the work of the rhythmic choir. Ever since Christmas programs progressed beyond the statuelike tableaux there has been experimentation in connection with the art of symbolic movement. It was in a Christmas pageant that I first attempted something of the kind simply by having angels, who stood in the background, lift their arms during the singing of the familiar lines of "Silent Night":

> With the angels let us sing,
> "*Alleluia*" to our King

People in the congregation sensed the aspiration of the "angels" who seemed drawn upward in adoration. The next year, after studying Renaissance paintings and sculpture, we created designs for parts of several carols where symbolic movement seemed a natural expression of reverence, dignity, and beauty.

If a Christmas pageant starts with a candlelight processional, "O Holy Night" by Adolphe Adam is a good selection to use. The "angels" walk slowly toward the worship center, reaching it in time to kneel at

> Fall on your knees

and then raise their candles evenly, with heads back and attention high above the tip of the candle flame during

> O hear the angel voices

When the art of the rhythmic choir is being introduced for the first time, it would be wise to present but one number and it should be slow, dignified, and reverent.

Carols were originally composed for movement (see p. 120) and certain ones seem to be natural mediums for rhythmic interpretation. The refrain of "Angels We Have Heard on High" suggests the possibility of variations in sweeping, wide turns during the "Gloria," ending with an upward reach, followed by kneeling, but still with a high focus during "in excelsis Deo." "What Child is This" has a two-part pattern that lends itself, in the verse, to simple progression or circling

of "angels," and, in the refrain, to joyous upward movements of exaltation. Another rhythmic interpretation of this carol is possible using three "angels." The first interprets the first verse and refrain. The second "angel" interprets the second verse and then the first two dance symbolically together during the second refrain of

> Nails, spears shall pierce Him through,
> The Cross be borne for me, for you.

At the beginning of the third verse, the third "angel" comes forward and the other two who have been kneeling, rise and follow her. They symbolize the three gift-bringers during the line

> So bring Him incense, gold, and myrrh

and continue the rhythmic interpretation to its climax of joy and adoration.

The composer of the carol "In Dulci Jubilo" dreamed that he saw angels dancing in adoration as they sang this lilting melody, and upon waking, he wrote down the tune. In the beautiful carols of the Renaissance period we find a real affinity for creative movement, which fits in well with Christmas pageants.

For a more advanced group there are sections of Handel's *Messiah* that provide dramatic music for rhythmic interpretation; starting with the passage "There were shepherds," continuing through the solo of the angel, also through the passage "Fear not," and then culminating with the sudden appearance of the Heavenly Host "praising God and saying,

'Glory to God!' " This great chorus can be interpreted by an interweaving of designs to correspond to the interweaving of the voice parts. The accented "good wills" and the quality of radiance present in The *Messiah* seem to invite symbolic expression.

LENT

To convey the Lenten message, the church has turned to the arts, especially to music. So the sister art of the rhythmic choir finds music expressive of the variety of experiences connected with Lent and with Holy Week in particular. The first Palm Sunday can be suggested by a simple choir processional down the main aisle of the church. If the choir, without anthem books, sings Faure's "The Palms" and proceeds with heads held high and the focus of attention on the worship center, the congregation will catch the mood of the first Palm Sunday processional. If palm branches or fronds are used, they can provide an added climax by being lifted as each choir member reaches the worship center. Especially on the "Hosanna's" it is effective to have branches lifted. A Palm Sunday hymn such as "All Glory, Laud and Honor" by Melchior Teschner (1615) or "Hosanna, Loud Hosanna" to music from Hartig's *Vollständige Sammlung* (1830) can be used instead of "The Palms" with a similar emphasis.

Good Friday has always drawn the interest of religious artists because of its dramatic intensity and its stirring message of redemption. In the *Seven Last Words*, Theodore Dubois brings out the bitterness of the mob when it cries out:

He is death guilty! He is death guilty!
Take him! Take him! Let us crucify him!

The addition of a rhythmic choir makes this part of the cantata more vivid by contributing a visual portrayal simultaneously with the auditory experience. With throbbing, angular movements the group presses forward. Skillful use of lighting which casts immense, menacing shadows, projects a vast mood of imminent violence. As the mob moves about restlessly with sharp and stylized gestures it expresses the callous words of

Be his blood on us and on our children!

Again it surges forward to the music of

He is death guilty!

But as a soloist sings

Then they did crucify Jesus and the two thieves,

those in the mob cower and their shadows are not visible. Gradually the single shadow-form of a man with outstretched arms emerges, high and lifted up. Soon after two similar shadows appear on either side as the soloist continues:

One at his left, the other at his right—

But the restless group has subsided only temporarily. Now it rushes forward again with its repeated pattern of criminal intent. As the mob comes together with violent, outstretched hands, the words of Jesus are heard,

Father, Father, forgive them, for they know not what they do.

Radiant light from above floods over them during these words, and they sink down slowly with attention drawn to the light, even as they cringe before it in fear and agony. They are beginning to comprehend what they have done.

This conflict between the powers of life and death can be expressed symbolically[1] to the music of Bach's "Christ Lay in the Bonds of Death." Two of the rhythmic choir form a cross: one stands in front with arms outstretched to the sides, the other stands directly behind with arms raised parallel, straight above her head. A third member of the group, as Life, expresses the serene joy of spiritual awareness. Soon a fourth member, as Death, appears, causes the Cross to be shattered and then struggles symbolically to dominate Life. However Life has the inner energy to triumph over Death. So Life raises the Cross and is joyously exultant. One stanza in this chorale describes this spiritual struggle:

It was a wondrous fight, I trow
That death's dominion rended.
Fast bound hath Life, His grim foe
And Death's long reign is ended.
As to us the scripture saith:
In death Christ hath conquered Death
With scorn Hell is now discrowned, Allelujah!

One of the simplest and yet most effective interpretations
for the Lenten season is of the hymn "When I Survey the
Wondrous Cross," to the music of an early Gregorian chant,
adapted by Lowell Mason. The portrayal of "The Three

Marys" is based on the reference in John 19:25 which tells of the presence of Mary, the Mother of Jesus, Mary Cleopas, and Mary Magdalen at the foot of the Cross. There was a dramatic presentation of the three Marys as early as the tenth century in the *Quem Quaeritus* in early liturgy. By the twelfth century this incident was interpreted symbolically with music, gestures and speech in the *Planctus* (see p. 109).

The twentieth century interpretation has a special depth and meaning of its own. The three Marys stand as a sculpturelike group in cloaks of gold, blue, and red. During the first stanza of "When I Survey the Wondrous Cross" the Mary in gold approaches the cross which is larger and higher than an altar cross. In sorrow, she kneels, rises, and with eyes upon the cross goes to the farther side and kneels with head slightly bowed. On the second stanza, Mary the Mother, in blue, comes forward. Her sorrow is expressed by more sweeping movements of grief. She kneels beside the cross on the nearer side. In the third stanza, Mary Magdalen, in red, comes to the center, lifts both arms, kneels, and with an opening movement, reveals her sorrow, leans back, and lowers her arms. It is Mary the Mother who rises first, then the others, and they turn as a group to leave. Their heads are up and they seem drawn together because of the sorrow which has given them a new spiritual bond. One value of this symbolic portrayal is that it has its wider parallel in everyday living: the individual acceptance of tragedy, the dedication to deeper spiritual living, and the strengthened sense of fellowship with others who have also experienced "the dark night of the soul."

EASTER

It is Easter that calls for every art of the church to express the wonder and joy of the Risen Christ. So the rhythmic choir finds both the message and the music ready for joyous expression. The well-known hymn "Christ the Lord is Risen Today, Alleluia," is easily interpreted in solo form as if the angel at the tomb is revealing the joy of the Risen Christ. There are many Easter anthems with variety of rhythms and emphasis and with deep dramatic quality. A rhythmic choir should become thoroughly familiar with an anthem and then gradually create its own symbolic patterns. "We will be merry far and wide, on this most holy Easter-tide, Alleluia," is an anthem originally by Praetorius of the sixteenth century and recently arranged by Ralph E. Marryott. The interweaving of the voice parts suggests that there could be a visualization with this pattern as its base and the costumes in four shades to correspond to the four voice parts of the anthem. This musical selection has many joyous "alleluias" which provide for sweeping turns and upward movements of exaltation. In this anthem there are sections which are reminiscent of sixteenth century carols, and other parts which suggest processionals; so it offers an unusual variety of rhythms in its expression of Easter gladness. Other joyous anthems are Gaul's "Russian Easter Alleluia," and Mozart's "Alleluia." These are rather fast in tempo and call for more technical ability, but they are not too difficult. The beautiful hymn, "Alleluia, the Strife is O'er" by Palestrina (c. 1551) offers a slower rhythm in its expression of religious joy, and can be as effective as more complicated compositions.

With this art of the rhythmic choir there may be a new and modern approach to Easter pageantry. Erika Thimey (see p. 178) created an "Easter Story" dance-drama concerned with the struggle between light and darkness. Into the darkness of tragedy comes illumination of spiritual truth, and with this, a new life expressed in joyful movements.

Although the pageants of Christmas and Easter offer opportunities for the use of creative and symbolic movement, there are other areas where this art can be of service to the church.

Worship Interpretations

The rhythmic choir can help to make the act of worship an experience of consecration. In expressing worship it may employ a number of arts: the sculptured lines of the body and of the group formations; the pictorial grace of colorful, flowing costumes; the harmony of great religious music; and the mystic sense of the self lost in adoration.

> If you get simple beauty and naught else
> You get about the best things God invents.[2]

In the worship numbers, the rhythmic choir moves with a disciplined simplicity that radiates spiritual beauty. These devotional numbers should be given as a part of a worship service. "The Religious Dance must express meditation, prayer and praise so naturally, as never to appear as an irrelevant illustration which would break up the continuity of worship . . . It should be done in the church as an integral part of some religious office—working not to a climax of surprise, but to one instead, of solemn and thrilling recognition of what is by common tradition, sacred."[3]

The processional can be used as a "call to worship," the rhythmic choir coming down the aisle can be symbolic of the congregation's centering its thought on coming together to worship. Then comes the kneeling, symbolic of humility, and the upward reach, expressive of aspiration and the seeking of spiritual power. Music which lends itself to the use of gestures of worship is found in such anthems as Gounod's "Sanctus" and Handel's "Holy Art Thou," and also in such hymns as "Worship the Lord in the Beauty of Holiness" (first two stanzas), "Just as I Am," "Day is Dying in the West," "I Need Thee Every Hour," and "Sweet Hour of Prayer" (first two stanzas).

A processional with candles brings an added beauty to a vesper service. The carrying of candles symbolizes the bringing of the light of faith to a service of devotion. Gradually as the candles are placed in tall candelabra the chancel becomes radiant. If Bortniansky's "Cherubim Song" is used, about two-thirds of the music will cover the candle processional. There is a natural break in the anthem where the "Amen" appears; following that, the music increases in tempo and volume. The rhythmic choir having placed the candles, is now free to express inspired dedication, followed by a quieter period of meditation and then to conclude in a mood of spiritual exaltation in whirling "alleluias."

The rhythmic choir may be divided into two groups and

offer alternating designs that come together at the climax of the worship experience. The Bach chorale, "Jesu, Joy of Man's Desiring" provides such a pattern for a divided group—one being the worshipers who move only during the singing sections, and the other being the circling choir that runs smoothly to the accompaniment between the vocal sections. The choreography for this chorale is written out in the Appendix.

Prayer may be expressed in symbolic movement. The Lord's Prayer can be interpreted with reverent simplicity to the music by Malotte. Evelyn Broadbent's choreography for this has been used and adapted by rhythmic choirs in a number of churches and youth conferences in New England.

Using Bizet's "Agnus Dei" with the beauty of this prayerful music, a group can discover many designs of prayer symbolized. While the group is kneeling in silent prayer, an occasional individual may rise and move as if in prayer for the others. The seeking of compassion may be represented by the wide swing of a downstage arm as the group stands in a V-shaped line (see frontispiece). Hands peaked together, then opening out, suggest the seeking and openness to spiritual power. A wide circle back to back with arms at shoulder height, palms up, finger tips touching those of the nearest ones—expresses the prayerful concern for the whole world:

> Thou that takest away the world's guilt
> Have compassion upon us, and grant us thy peace.

"My Faith Looks Up to Thee" is a prayer hymn, the first three verses of which can be interpreted with various symbolic

gestures. The wide outward sweep of the arm suggests "Take all my guilt away." "Strengthen to my fainting heart" can be illustrated by a serene walk with head up, one arm raised high as if pointing the way. During "As thou hast died for me," the group may kneel while two in the center form a living cross (one member facing right with right arm extended forward at shoulder height, the other member standing directly in front facing left with right arm extending forward at shoulder height, and the left arm raised perpendicularly). "A living fire" can be envisaged by a close circling of the group with the inside arms extended high and the fingers pointing up. "While life's dark maze I tread" suggests the historical labyrinth dance (see p. 111). A rhythmic choir can give an impression of a maze by progressive figure-eight designs, similar to a "grand chain," but with arms outstretched shoulder high and passing back to back. This interweaving objective pattern projects the idea of walking isolated, as if in a maze. At the conclusion of the third stanza, the group comes together in a high peak of adoration during the singing:

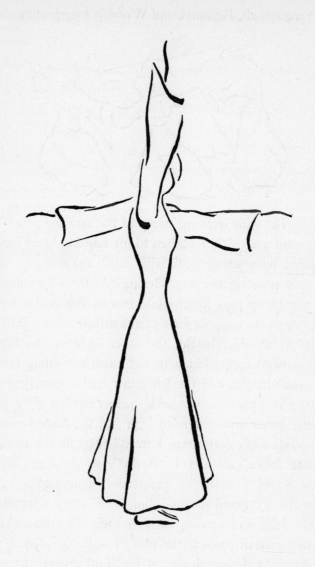

Nor let me ever stray, from Thee aside.

These suggestions of designs may help the reader to visualize some of the symbolic beauty that may reinforce the intellectual concept of prayer and worship. If the reader plans to create some religious dances, these suggestions may be considered as simple tools. The art of the rhythmic choir should not be hampered by imitation, but should be the creative work of each group. A rhythmic choir of young people will spend hours developing the symbolic movements that fit the mood and the music. And when they present their interpretation in a service of worship, it will be their complete act of consecration.

CHAPTER VII

Dramatize Religious Ideas Through This Art

Dance-dramas

As DRAMA is used in the writings of the Bible, in religious music, and in preaching, so the rhythmic choir may illustrate religious truths or problems in a dramatic way. Unless a church has come to feel at home with the new art of the rhythmic choir, it is wise to present dance-dramas in the parish hall rather than in the church sanctuary. Some churches of a more liturgical tradition may feel that the stage is the best location for all rhythmic choir presentations.

The religious dance is an art form and, as such, can be selective as to the specific scenes portrayed. A sculptor does not try to tell a whole story, but chooses a mood or incident which fits the medium in which he is working. As Martha Graham has said, "Artistry lies in restraint as much as in expression."[1]

Men in Dance-Dramas

Many rhythmic choir numbers are effective with girls alone but in dance-dramas there is need for the strength that men provide. The Prodigal Son, Job, and Boaz should be portrayed

by men. An increasing number of schools—for example, the University of Wisconsin, Oberlin College, and Hampton Institute—have men in modern dance classes.

That men should appear in the dances of the early Christian church was even more to be expected than the participation of women. Most angels were represented as males both in the scriptures and in the traditional art of the church. The twentieth century Christian church, which has been through a period of overfeminized art, could well afford to use men when there are masculine parts. In Robert Storer's "Christmas Masque" young men in green jerkins come down the aisle with laurel wreaths and swing them in a patterned, rhythmic motion.

Biblical Dramas

In both the Old and the New Testaments there are dra
matic stories that can be interpreted by rhythmic choirs. A
few that have been worked out for church presentation wil
be described.

In "The Prodigal Son," there might be an introductor
scene in the home, as in the interpretation by the Jooss Ballet
but with the rhythmic choir in Hanover the scene begins afte
the Prodigal has departed. Before he appears on a raised plat
form upstage, grotesque forms as "vices" mill about on th
main floor. The Prodigal rejoices in his freedom. As he come
down onto the stage the "vices" surge up to meet him. Th
seven "vices" try to attract the Prodigal Son, who approache
one, then another, and finally pursues them as they dash off
Lighting effects throw the shadows of the "vices" against th
wall and intensify the mood. The first part of Sibelius' "E
Saga" is an effective musical background for this action. In th
following scene, a low central spotlight magnifies the shadov
of the forlorn Prodigal into gigantic proportions. His despai
is symbolized by four "remorses," in shapeless costumes an
hoods of black jersey. Their angular gestures are also amplifie
by shadow effects. To the accompaniment of the last half o
Sibelius' "Swan of Tuonela," the "remorses," who have move
to its relentless beat, gradually fade into the background. Th
Prodigal Son rises with an inner peace which has been purifie
by humility. He turns to go to his father as the music rein
forces this mood of decisive moral renewal.

The dramatic story of "Job: the Perennial Problem of Suffering" can be deeply moving. Here a strong, masculine lead
is required for the part of Job. The messenger and the three
friends should be men also, especially if the story is presented
in modern costume. However, if the traditional Palestinian
cloaks and headdress are used, women can take these parts.
Because the problems of Job seem to be perennial, the Hanover group decided to present the story in basic, simple cos-
tuming, not Palestinian. William Blake's illustrations of *The
Book of Job* were used as guides for certain dramatic group-

ings. A Dartmouth student, John Lothrop, working closel
with the dancers, created the choreographic music. Since th
approach was psycho-religious, neither Satan nor God had
visible part. The succession of scenes included the serenit
of Job and his wife; Job's acceptance of the messenger's new
of the loss of his possessions and his children; the bearing o

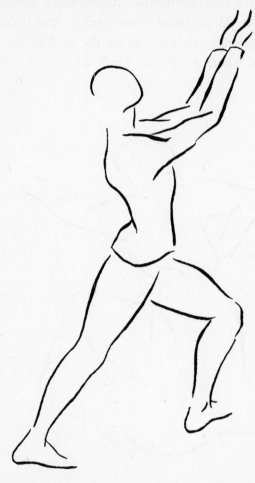

physical suffering; and the three friends' arguments that Job
must have sinned because a just God would not permit so
much evil otherwise. The closing scene revealed the deeper
awareness of God that Job achieved, going beyond moral

equations to a new humility and release which lifted him into radiant light. All of these inner conflicts and insights were expressed through the medium of the modern dance, with most of the choreography by Linda Lion who also danced

the part of Job's wife. The fact that four Dartmouth College students were willing to work out the portrayal of this prob

lem-drama reflects the truth expressed by Ted Shawn that "Until big themes, religious themes, cosmic themes, become again considered as the natural and rightful field of the dance, men capable of doing big things will not see in the dance an opportunity for great art expression."[2] Religious dance-dramas call for men of strength, genuineness, and conviction.

The story of Ruth is another Biblical drama that lends itself to creative interpretation, especially enhanced by the dramatic music of César Franck's cantata "Ruth." To hear this music is to feel the stirring possibilities it has for visual presentation. The following selections can be used for certain scenes: (1) The Farewell Chorus of Moabites, Trio of Naomi Ruth, and Orpah; (2) Chorus of the Bethlehemites welcoming Naomi and Ruth; (3) The Chorus of the Reapers, the Meeting of Ruth and Boaz; and (4) the Prophetic Conclusion, the Union of Ruth and Boaz, and the Wedding Chorus

Dramatic Conflicts (Non-Biblical)

Dance dramas do not need to be Bible-centered, but can deal with religious insights into conflicts of our times.

"True Freedom" illustrates the use of dance-drama to proclaim religious truth in meeting conflicts and problems. This dance drama has five episodes with narration preceding each section:

Episode I: Humanity in Bondage, Searching for True Freedom

The humanity group (thirteen dancers), in costumes of deep blue, maroon, green, and gold, comes down the aisle with arms crossed shoulder high to the accompaniment of a monotonous march. The narrator has just read:

> On and on comes humanity,
> Searching for true freedom;
> On and on comes humanity,
> Searching, but in bondage to itself.

Occasionally the music breaks into searching cadences and the rhythmic choir pauses to reach high from side to side, with hands clasped tightly together. When all of the group reaches the chancel or the stage their clasped hands come down on their necks like yokes that are too heavy to bear. So the group becomes crushed and slowly kneels.

Episode II: Spokesmen for Freedom Rejected

> Two arise as spokesmen for freedom.
> They proclaim:
> "Guard political freedom!
> Maintain freedom of the press!
> Encourage religious freedom!
> Protect freedom of speech!"
> But humanity continues its self-centered routine.
> When it does heed these appeals
> Humanity turns upon these freedoms
> With antagonism and mockery.

The group now rises and starts to pace back and forth with complete indifference to each other and to two spokesmen who have ascended platforms at either side upstage. They try to reach humanity to warn it to safeguard various freedoms. Some of the group stop for an instant, but then continue their self-centered pattern. When their attention is finally arrested, figures symbolic of various antagonistic viewpoints ascend the platforms and crush the spokesmen down toward the center. Immediately the whole group taunts them with movements of ridicule and mockery. They pause, converged upon the two spokesmen who are crouching as if toward off the group.

Episode III: Organization to Gain Security Fails

> Two project their plans for freedom.
> They proclaim:
>> "Organize to produce! Produce! Produce!
>> Secure for yourselves freedom from want!
>> Organize to defend! Defend! Defend!
>> Insure for yourselves freedom from fear
>>   and freedom from oppression!"
> But humanity finds itself in bondage to
>   mechanical organization.
> In its frenzy for total defense,
> It drives itself to chaos—
> Chaos and darkness.

These organizers begin to bring order out of the confusion by forming two rows of the humanity group who face each

ther. The organizers set up a monotonous movement symbolic of production, as if the groups were working mechanical
presses. The left arm swings forward and up to a vertical
position, then down, and immediately the right hand crosses
to the left hand and back to the neighbor's left hand, as if

here were a long assembly belt. The palms of the hands are
parallel to the floor as if resting on an assembly line. Over
and over the vertical and horizontal movements are repeated,
as the two lines gradually pivot to form one single line. Sud-
denly, as the music changes from its monotonous beat to
strident and piercing chords, alternate members of the group
lunge forward violently, while the others push upward fran-
ically. The fingers are extended intensely as the forward-
lunging figures alternate to the right and left as if warding
off threatening attack. The music increases in tempo and the

group movements become rushed and chaotic, ending with
humanity falling to the floor. A blackout increases the mood
of despair, but a spotlight, centered on the cross, brings a
radiant gleam.

Episode IV: Revelation of Christ

> Out of the darkness shines the light of the cross,
> The Cross of Christ.
> Hear His words for humanity
> That strives to find freedom
> Through ways that have no unity:
> "Seek ye first the Kingdom of Heaven
>   and its righteousness,
> And all these things shall be added unto you."
> "If ye abide in my word, then ye are truly my
>   disciples, and ye shall know the truth, and
>   the truth shall make you free."

A group of five, in white costumes, representing Christianity,
ascend the platform and kneel before the cross, then rise to
express adoration as the music of interweaving "alleluias"
is sung.

Episode V: Christianity Brings True Freedom

> But Christianity is more than adoration.
> As Christ came to bring the abundant life to all,
> So Christianity reaches out to the fearful,
> To the disillusioned, and to the embittered,
> And points the way to the will of God.
> In joining to seek His will,
> Humanity finds True Freedom.

The representatives of Christianity go among those who symbolize fallen humanity; of these, four rise and rush fearfully
away, but are drawn back as the "Christians" make wide move-

nents pointing toward the cross. As they return, three others
of the fallen ones rise from their despair and bondage, which
changes to release and vision as the "Christians" part the hands
which had been clenched. As the "Christians" dance with spir-
tual joy the released ones echo their movements. Six others
who are resentful and defensive move with sharp and bitter
gestures. The palms of their hands in a vertical position express their rejection of any assistance, even though the "Chris-

tians" try to point them to a higher focus. As the resentful ones pause, two of the Christian group express their awareness of the wholeness of life with wide, circling movements and turns. When they approach each of the resentful ones with an upward surge of movement the defensive gestures are transformed by the lifting of the hands and the raising of the head.

All of humanity has now caught the vision of true freedom based on personal commitment and loyalty to Christ. The Christianity and humanity groups are drawn into a wide outer circle and a peaked inner circle as the singing choir bursts into glorious "alleluias." After the circling designs, they all gradually ascend the platform below the cross. On the closing "alleluia," as if from a deep inner impulse, they reach up, lost in a loyalty beyond themselves.

Perhaps the reader, following these sketchy clues, has been able to visualize imaginatively the development of a religious dance-drama. On the other hand, he may have found this very unsatisfactory. To describe scenes from a dance-drama through the medium of words is as difficult as a verbal description of a series of sculptural masterpieces such as the Parthenon frieze, Michelangelo's "Pietà," or Lorado Taft's "March of Time." If the imaginative visualization is quite different from the way this dance drama was actually performed, that is quite unimportant. This rough sketch of the development of one dance-drama has been made in the hope that others may use similar methods to interpret their own ideas, and so bring new religious awareness to people.

Dance-dramas often need the assistance of composers. The

rhythmic choir in Hanover could not have presented "True Freedom" without the assistance of William Yakovac, a student at Dartmouth College in 1945, who was willing to experiment in the field of choreographic music. As in the dance-drama of "Job," the problem, if suitable music is not available, is to find a composer who will work with a rhythmic choir. This should not be undertaken until the group has learned to work together over a period of time and has established a common understanding of its techniques and aims.

The rhythmic choir can assist general dramatic productions by providing choral interpretations of certain moods, conflicts, or aspirations. This use of a rhythmic choir is similar to the choirs which danced and spoke in the classical Greek dramas. Miss Helen Kromer, in her religious drama, *Chain Reaction* (presented at the International Congregational Council, June, 1949), chose a rhythmic choir to set the mood and symbolism of the chain reactions of evil and good. As a choral dance of evil, the group, costumed in black, against a back lighting of red, combined spoken words with action. As they lunged for-

ward as if to project evil, individual voices, in the staccato rhythm of the dance pattern, shouted such lines as:

> Hiroshima, bombed into dust!
> A band of Moslems kill a Hindu!

Later, as the fury increased, there were single cries of:

> Hatred!
> Starvation!
> Destruction!
> Killing!
> Death!

To illustrate the chain reaction of good, a rhythmic choir group in white costumes formed interlinking patterns. Each one had a special thought which she expressed in words while moving slowly in a symbolic design to the music of Bortniansky's "Cherubim Song." One such speech was:

> A Christian laywoman in India is
> taught to read by Laubach's method
> and teaches the people in her village.

This use of the choral dance intensified moods and at the same time was an integral part of a complete dramatic presentation.

CHAPTER VIII

Religious Television Needs Symbolic Movement

TELEVISION depends on two things for its success: a scene with movement and accompanying sound. Speech alone and music alone, which are the common channels for radio, and for many church services, are no longer adequate for the new art involved in television. Will the churches face the problem of adjusting the sermon-preaching and the choir-singing type of worship service to fit the requirements of visual interest? Television asks worship to change from its static conventionality. "To give movement to worship is to awaken it," Harold Ehrensperger states. "When the worship of God becomes the expression of the entire person, it is not a static, motionless thing. The mind is alive, the emotions are aroused, and physical expression becomes as natural as does any action that results from religious conviction." Effective religious television programs need to show this revelation of conviction.

As more and more television sets are purchased, it becomes increasingly urgent that the church re-examine the programs it brings into the homes. Is the church considering the millions of children, youth and adults who observe television programs? Are there programs of spiritual beauty and Christian significance on Sundays, or are there only sports and light entertainments? Church groups can present effective religious dramas, and they can present social problems in informal semidramatic ways, but what will they do about projecting worship? The beauty of Christian worship must not be pushed off the television programs. If the churches will experiment with the art of symbolic movement in religious telecasts, families will gather together around their television sets to watch religious interpretations. Young people will turn to such programs because the art of the rhythmic choir is so largely a contribution of youth. Instead of religion being presented through long moral verbalizations, it can appear in a new, dynamic, experiential dimension of a visual art.

Symbolic movements add beauty and vitality to a worship service presented over television. During a prayer, there may be a closeup of praying hands with gradual variations in symbolic gestures. Parts of some hymns or anthems can be portrayed with interpretive designs by a rhythmic choir. While the Scripture is read, it can be illustrated with symbolic movement, as in Psalm 27 or I Corinthians 13; or parts of the Scripture may be read in sections with rhythmic interpretations interspersed, as in the story of "The Prodigal Son" or "Ruth." All of these interpretive possibilities should not be presented in one service of worship but are suggested as symbolic portrayals for occasional religious telecasts. Of course the sermon must be brief, but people will listen if they know it is to be for five or ten minutes, and not a half hour. The sermon may become a more precious element in a service of worship because it will be like a pearl of great price.

When the rhythmic choir of Hanover gave a presentation over the WPIX Television Chapel, the religious director

wrote of it as "a remarkable, beautiful and impressive program." Dr. Scotford wrote in his article "Television Takes Work" in *Advance*, April, 1949, concerning this telecast: "Everyone was impressed by the beauty of the dances and the reverent atmosphere of the broadcast." At another time, when the New Haven Council of Churches sponsored a television program on "The Spiritual Use of Creative Movement," using the rhythmic choir of Hanover, Mr. Stanley Knock, Jr., director of Religious Television, wrote that the Council of Churches presented the program as a venture in religious expression, and he continued, "We are now sure that this type of religious telecasting is definitely acceptable for inter-denominational groups. We highly recommend it to all who wish to spread the message of Jesus Christ to a large segment of the population in such a manner as to be compelling and convincing."

There is an urgent need for adventurous and imaginative spirits to encourage directors of religious television programs to use more of this symbolic art. Perhaps the times to start experimenting with this art are at Christmas and Easter when the use of pageantry is accepted so widely. Then, gradually, various types of symbolic interpretation may be used in other worship services. Television can be a lever for a new type of evangelism if the directors feel the concern and backing of church groups in experimenting with this new art.

CHAPTER IX

The History of This Art in the Christian Church

FROM its beginning the Christian Church has used symbolic movements and gestures which at times were put into choreographic form. Little is known of their exact nature and there has been no complete gathering of references. But the collection of choreographic descriptions that follows suggests that sacred dances were widely known and used in the Christian Church.

The First Five Centuries

Although the New Testament has no direct reference to the sacred dance, there seems to be no aversion to the use of the dance as an accepted expression of joy. A remark of Jesus, "We have piped unto you, and ye have not danced" (Matt. 11:17) would indicate that Jesus was not against dancing, but recognized it as a normal means of expressing joy. Similarly, in his story about the rejoicing over the return of the Prodigal Son, he mentions that there was dancing (Luke 15:25).

Paul reminds the early Christians that their *bodies are the temples of the Holy Spirit* and that they should glorify God in their bodies as well as in their spirits (I Cor. 6:19.20).

97

That manual action was a part of prayer expression is clearly expressed in Paul's letter to Timothy: "I will therefore that men pray everywhere, *lifting up holy hands,* without wrath or doubt" (I Tim. 2:8). So we gather that Paul respected the body as a channel for religious expression.

As late as the fifth century there are isolated references to Paul as one who had been interested in some form of the sacred dance. Chrysostom (*c.* 387) wrote of the Christians at Antioch celebrating the New Year's festival in a spiritual way by spending a large part of the time *dancing with Paul.* They had danced spiritual dances in decent order, had shared in the cup overflowing with spiritual discipline, and made themselves pipes and harps for the spirit to play on.[1]

Theodoret (*c.* 430) referred to Paul as "one who had seen the beauty of Paradise and the dances of the holy ones."[2] This vision of Paradise with angels dancing has persisted throughout the centuries.

A circling dance of the disciples around Jesus is described in the apocryphal Acts of John written about A.D. 120. It is called the "Hymn of Jesus":

Now before he was taken by the lawless Jews, he gathered all of us together and said, "Before I am delivered up unto them let us sing an hymn to the Father, and so go forth to that which lieth before us." He bade us therefor make, as it were a ring, holding one another's hands, and himself standing in the midst, he said, "Answer Amen unto me." He began then to sing an hymn and to say:
  "Glory be to the Father."
  And we, going about in a ring, answered him: Amen.
  "Glory be to thee, word: Glory be to thee, Grace. Amen.
  I would be saved, and I would save. Amen.

Grace danceth. I would pipe; dance ye all. Amen.
I would mourn: lament ye all. Amen.
The number Eight singeth praise with us. Amen.
The number Twelve danceth on high. Amen.
The whole on high hath part in our dancing. Amen.
Who so danceth not, knoweth not what cometh to pass.
I would be united, and I would unite. Amen.
A door am I to thee that knockest at me. Amen.
Now answer thou unto my dancing.
Behold thyself in me who speak, and seeing what I do, keep
    silence about my mysteries.
Thou that dancest, perceive what I do, for there is this passion of
    the manhood, which I am about to suffer. For thou couldst
    not at all have understood what thou sufferest, if I had not
    been sent unto thee, as the word of the Father. Thou that
    sawest what I suffer sawest me as suffering, and seeing it thou
    didst not abide but wert wholly moved. Who I am, thou
    shalt know when I depart. Learn thou to suffer, and
    thou shalt be able not to suffer. I would keep tune with holy
    souls. Do thou understand the whole, and having understood
    it, say: Glory be to the Father. Amen."
Thus having danced with us the Lord went forth.

G.R.S. Mead in *The Sacred Dance* suggests that this hymn is an ancient mystery-ritual of early Christendom. "It is the sacred dance of the *Unio mystica* wherein the new born disciple is united with the Master." As indicated in the Acts of John, the group slowly circles round making a "mystic circle" and to each statement by Christ in the center there is the response, "Amen." Augustine (*c.* 400) in a letter to the Spanish Bishop Ceretius says that this "Hymn of Jesus" was used through the fourth century by many heretical schools, including the followers of Priscillian of the Gnostic movement. Because this "Hymn of Jesus" is in the apocryphal New Testament it was not included in later traditional Christian literature. However, it reveals that religious dances were employed in the second century.

The Christian Gnostics also had a "labyrinthine dance" which interpreted the "Naassene Hymn" in which the human soul is described as "wandering in the labyrinth of ills."[3] The Saviour descends bringing the Gnosis which frees the soul and leads her out of the labyrinth. In the well-known hymn, "My Faith Looks Up to Thee," Ray Palmer visualizes in a similar way the soul in a maze or labyrinth:

> When life's dark maze I tread,
> And griefs around me spread,
> Be Thou my Guide.

The *Didachè* (a short manual of church life and morals, written in A.D. 150) mentions a dance called "The Cosmic Mystery of the Church,"[4] which dealt with the mystery of the creation and involved a rhythmic interpretation of the sun, moon, stars, and planets.

Various church leaders in the third century wrote of the sacred dance as a commendable form of expression for religious feeling. To Clement of Alexandria (c. 195) as to any contemporary versed in Greek philosophy, what was regular, rhythmical, harmonious, was also in some sense, divine. So he wrote of "those who have not yet been initiated in the mysteries or have no taste for dance and song" as being like that which is "dissonant, unrhythmical and material" and so "must still stand out from the divine *chorós*."[5] Origen (c. 225) mentions a hymn with the line: "of the stars dancing in heaven for the salvation of the universe."[6] This hymn might have been connected with the "Cosmic Mystery of the Church" since it deals with the same subject. Gregory Thaumaturqus (*c.* 273) thought of the dance as a natural and spontaneous way of expressing religious joy. On the Feast of the Annunciation he declared, "Today Adam is renewed and dances with the angels, soaring to heaven."[7] He also expressed the joy of John the Baptist in this way: "Dance with me Jordan River, and leap with me, and set thy waves in rhythm, for thy maker has come to thee in body."[8]

Circling around a spiritual center is described by the Egyptian neo-platonist Plotinus (*c.* 244). He writes: "If, then, a soul is conscious of itself, it knows that its natural motion is in a circle not something external to itself, but round a centre in itself. Now the centre is that from which the circle is. . . . It does not yearn for us, so as to move round us, but we yearn after It, so as to move round It and ever round It, although we do not always keep our eyes on It. But as a *chorós* may sing out of tune when turned to face the play or audience, and then when it turns to the *chorós* leader, sings well and dances truly round him; so we for ever keep our eyes on Him, but when we do, then do we win to Perfectness and Peace and are no longer out of tune, but truly *dance round Him the Dance Divine*."[9] Also in Egypt, the Meletians,[10] followers of Bishop Mélèce (*c.* 326) of Lycopolis, had the custom of dancing while singing their hymns, clapping their hands, and striking numerous bells. To this day there are religious dances among the Coptic Christians in Egypt.

Men and women took part in circling and processional

religious dances in the fourth century. Eusebius (c. 304) states that Philo (in his essay *On the Contemplative Life* (c. A.D. 26)) describes a sacred all-night festival that was the same as that of the church in Eusebius' time.[11] "They first form two *chorói*, one of men and the other of women, and a leader is chosen for each; they then chant hymns composed in God's honour in many metres and melodies, sometimes one *chorós* beating the measure with their hands for the antiphonal chanting of the other, now dancing to the measure, at times dancing in procession, at times set dances and then circle dances going right and left."[12] This festal dance commemorated the triumphant dance of the Israelites after their miraculous passage through the Red Sea. Philo continues, "When the men and women together form one *chorós*, they sing hymns of joyful thanks to God the Saviour. Then Moses the prophet leads the men, and Miriam, the prophetess leads the women." So we see how in Eusebius' own words "dances and hymns taught them of God."[13]

David's dancing (II Samuel 6:14) seemed to be a well-known guide for sacred dancing. Gregory of Nyssa (c. 365) felt that David's dance signified "intense joy" and that he "by the rhythmic motions of his body thus showed in public his inner state of soul."[14] Gregory of Nazianzen (c. 369) described the Dance of David before the Ark as "that swift course of revolution manifold ordained by God."[15]

To "dance to the honor of God" as an exercise "worthy of an Emperor and of a Christian" was urged by Gregory, the Bishop of Constantinople. He held the dance in such respect that he reproached the Emperor Julian (successor to Constantine) for the bad use he (Julian) made of it: "If you are fond of dancing, if your inclination leads you to these festivals, dance as much as you like. But why revive before our eyes the dissolute dances of Herodias and the pagans. Rather, perform the dances of King David before the Ark; *dance to the honor of God.* Such exercises of peace and piety are worthy of an emperor and of a Christian."[16] Basil, (*c.* 369) Bishop of Caesarea, refers to the "angelic dance round God,"[17] and calls those happy who can imitate such dancing. Bishop Ambrose, (*c.* 385) advising his followers to dance like David, writes: "The dancing desired of the Lord is the dance of David before the Ark. Dancing should not be the companion of 'delight,' but of 'grace.' "[18]

Pantomimic dances and dramatic hymns were introduced into the liturgy and were received with enthusiasm. Arius had included a program of pantomimic dances commemorating the crucifixion in a liturgy called "Thalia." Athanasius, his opponent, recognized the value of these liturgical additions and from the fourth century on there were more opportunities for dramatic presentations.[19]

That the Christians at Antioch danced in church and before martyrs tombs is revealed in the writings of Theodosius (*c.* 386).[20] They had in Antioch a sacred festival, a *Chorostasia,* which was in imitation of angelic dancing. Chrysostom (*c.* 387) writes concerning it: "Of those in heaven and upon earth a unison is made—one general assembly, one single service of thanksgiving, one single transport of rejoicing, *one joyous dance.*"[21]

"Dance to the glory of God" is Chrysostom's advice as he holds before the Christians the example of David's religious dances. He refers them to pictures which show David "surrounded with his *Chorói* of prophets who in manifold modes and figures . . . sing, play instruments and *dance to the glory of God*."[22] He also warned them not to use "unseemly motions"[23] but decent gestures. Aware of pagan dancing, he urged Christians to keep their dances sacred, reminding them that God had not given them feet for such (i.e. pagan) dancing, but that they might "dance with the angels."[24]

To show thanksgiving to God, the early Christians had "accustomed dances." In a homily, written at the close of the fourth century, on the anniversary of the martyrdom of St. Polyeuctus, there are these words: "By what thanksgiving shall we acknowledge the love he had for God? If you wish, let us celebrate in his honor the accustomed dances."[25]

It was Augustine (*c.* 394) whose warning to keep the sacred dances disciplined was more severe. He was against "frivolous or unseemly"[26] dances. However he did not seem to object to dancing at sacred festivals.[27] Regrettable abuses had crept into sacred choreography at the early "Agapés." The Council of Gangres in 320 made an effort to reform the "Agapés," but it was not until the pontificate of Gregory the Great at the end of the sixth century that these abuses became controlled.

"Dancing in heaven"[28] was the occupation of the angels in the vision of Theodoret (*c.* 430). When he wrote about the martyrs he could see them in "their dance in the indestructible aeons." He urged his readers to follow their example that they might share in this dance, for they had been promised "the kingdom of the heavens and life that hath no end, and light intelligible, and to dance in company with those free of all body."[29] Here certainly would be the religious dance in its most spiritual form. Theodoret conceived of the sacred dance as a dance of the virtues in harmony with the powers above. What a change occurred in later centuries when the dance came to be considered the occupation of the vices in connection with the power of evil!

The dance seemed to be a spiritual medium of salvation for those in the fiery furnace (Daniel 3). Referring to the "Song of the Blessed Children" which described the story in Daniel, Theodoret wrote: "They summon to the dance both heaven and the waters above the heavens, and the powers that circle round the divine throne."[30] The flames of the burning fiery furnace were turned miraculously into dew, "so that those Blessed Children danced the dance in their midst, and sang the hymn."[31]

During the first five centuries of the Christian era, we see that the dance was recognized by the church as a natural way of expressing *joy*, a way of *salvation* and a way of *adoration*, as illustrated by the references to the dances of the holy ones, the martyrs, and the angels. The early Christians expressed in symbolic movement the deep joy that they felt in the coming of Christ, in the immortal life which the martyrs had earned and in the close spiritual bond between heaven and earth.

Their faith was not just an intellectual acceptance of certain beliefs, it was an experience of the abundant life and of spiritual joy.

The Early Middle Ages (A.D. 500–1100)

The period from the sixth to the twelfth century was marked by various crosscurrents. The church became more authoritarian and started to regulate all forms of religious activity. It began to legislate against some of the dances. Although there are occasional references to councils and papal authorities which opposed some religious dancing, it is difficult to know whether these disciplinary measures should be considered indicative of the total attitude or as valid judgment against religious dances which had degenerated. Certainly the sacred dance was a form of religious expression that the people appreciated. During this period, when the general culture was not stimulating, the church preserved and fostered the religious arts. It was at this time that the Mass developed with its definite, prescribed, symbolic movements to the accompaniment of Gregorian Chants.

The Alexandrian monk, Kosmas (c. 550) in his painting of The Cosmos[32] not only depicted his idea of the universe with the sun, moon, and stars about the earth, but also suggested rhythmic movement in the circling positions of the angels who held the stars and within the circle two angels carrying the sun and moon around the earth. It may be that his painting of angels in symbolic movement had a relation to the dance of the cosmic mystery of creation mentioned in the *Didaché*.

It was customary to celebrate festivals and saints' days with some form of dancing. On the vigil of a saint's day, or a day of prayer, silence, and penance, of course dancing was not suitable to the penitential spirit. So the edict of 589 by the Third Council of Toledo forbidding dancing in the churches during the vigil of saints' days was justifiable.[33]

In the next century, the Council of Toledo suggested that St. Isidore, the archbishop of Seville, present a "ritual rich in sacred choreography."[34] This ritual became incorporated into a holy Mass known as *Mozarabe*. It was used in the seven churches of Toledo and is still celebrated today in the cathedral of Seville. In the fifteenth century, Pope Eugenius II ordered this dance by the choir boys (or *seises*) to be discontinued. However, some ingenious persons managed to bring the *seises* to Rome, where they performed their dance before the Pope. After seeing it he permitted it to continue. So even today at Seville the dance is given three times a year—on Shrove Tuesday, the Feast of Corpus Christi, and the Feast of the Immaculate Conception. The traditional dance design is as follows: ten choir boys in antique red costumes sing and dance around the lectern and before the high altar; they form a line and play their castanets; after repeating this whole design twice, they file out of the choir and the service is ended.[35]

Sacred dances continued to spread during the eighth and ninth centuries, but there were efforts to restrain degenerate forms that were appearing. "That dancing was only attacked when seen in degraded form is evidenced by the Bull which the Pope Zacharias promulgated in 744 suppressing all *baladoires* or so-called 'religious dances,' because they were becoming degenerate. These were dances performed within the precincts of the cathedrals and churches at such times as Easter, Mid-summer and Christmas."³⁶ The midsummer festival was in honor of St. John and the dancing connected with it spread throughout Europe in the following centuries.

In an ancient liturgy of a Paris church, used about A.D. 900, a rubric reads: "Here the canon shall dance at the first Psalm." This might have involved some symbolic movements and gestures by the canon alone, or it may have pointed to a custom of the canon leading the choir boys in a circling design during the reading of the psalms.

The Flagellants appeared in northern Italy in the eleventh century and spread across to Germany and later to Spain and England. People of all classes and ages formed long processions which were headed by priests carrying crosses and banners. They walked through the streets in double file reciting prayers and drawing blood from their bodies by whipping themselves and each other with leather thongs. These exhibitions, symbolic of repentance, were suppressed somewhat, but have reappeared occasionally throughout the centuries, in various countries including Mexico and the United States. Martha Graham's dance, "El Penitente," which deals with the problem of sin, penance, and salvation, has a close relationship to the Flagellants.

Later Medieval Period (A.D. 1100–1500)

This was a period of dramatic and emotional expression. The church which had denounced the degenerate secular, theatrical productions, decided to create its own dramatic portrayals. It made a definite effort "to evoke public interest in the service of the church by the introduction of choral songs, of picturesque processionals, even of ceremonial dances performed in the choir."[37]

The *Planctus*[38] appears as a part of the Mass early in the twelfth century. This was a religious play concerned with the sorrows of the three Marys. The actions to accompany the lines and musical score were specified by interlinear indications in red, or "rubrics":

Magdalen: O brothers!
            (turns to the people with arms held out)
            Where is my hope?
            (beats her breast)
            Where is my consolation?
            (here raises her hands)
            Where is my whole salvation?
            (inclines her head, casts herself at Christ's feet)
            O Master Mine?
Virgin: O sorrow!
            (here points to Christ with open hands)
            Deep sorrow!
            Why, why indeed,
            (here points to Christ with open hands)
            Dear Son, hangest thou thus,
            Thou who art life
            (here beats her breast)
            And has forever been?

The third Mary followed with similar lines and actions. Later Mary, the Virgin, and Magdalen spoke together. They wore white or liturgical colors, with Magdalen probably in red. The actors were clergy, holy sisters or choir boys. The play was more chanted to music than spoken. Here in undeveloped form is that interrelation of gesture, music, verse and meaning which provides a base for future religious dancing.

Mystery and Miracle Plays began to take form at this time. Sometimes they were presented in the *ballatoria* (dancing pavement) which was a space in the front of the church or at the west door where awnings were hung. At other times they were transported and presented on wagon-stages. In France, England, and Germany there was a thriving interest in these plays, which included besides the dramatic action, the dancing of the follies, devils, and Salome. The follies, which represented the vices, tried to attract people in the audience; the devil, as the leading dancer, with his troupe of assisting devils, enjoyed scaring them; and the acrobatic dancing of Salome entertained them. On the porch at Rouen there is a bas-relief of Salome in an acrobatic dance position. It is evident that the dancing connected with these religious dramatizations was mainly theatrical and not sacred.

Monastic orders, during the twelfth and thirteenth centuries, seemed to find the dance of religious value when used in their disciplined groups. The monks of the Cistercian Order "danced and prayed for the salvation of the universe."[39] Also, the Franciscans sang and danced and called themselves the singing servants of Christ. Fra Jacapone da Todi (*c.* 1270), a Franciscan monk, wrote, "Oh that each one who loves the Lord would join in the dance, singing of his devotion."[40] Friar Marti of Alicante found time to write a treatise on dancing, even during the period of the Inquisition.[41] The nuns of Villaceaux celebrated the feasts of the Holy Innocents and Mary Magdalen with appropriate dances.[42]

There was careful planning in the use of sacred dances for

special holy days. Toward the middle of the twelfth century, Jean Beleth mentions four *tripudia* in use during the days following the Nativity season: that of the deacons on St. Stephen's Day, of the priests on St. John's Day, of the altar boys on Holy Innocents' Day, and finally that of the sub-deacons on Circumcision Day or the Epiphany. In the thirteenth century, Bishop Durand de Mende mentions the same distribution of ceremonies. Also in his *Rationale Divinorum Officiorum*, he writes, "They begin to conduct the choral dance." At Puy, when the clergy celebrated Circumcision Day, a rubric of the church, written in 1327, instructed the clergy, *de danser avec énergie à la fin de l'office de cette fête.*[43]

In Chartres Cathedral (*c.* 1200) there was built into the floor a maze (or labyrinth) which was forty feet across. "Labyrinths were not uncommon in medieval and perhaps more ancient churches. Pilgrims to Chartres still practice the devotion of the rosary on the labyrinth."[44] In an article in *The Catholic Encyclopedia* on "Labyrinths" we find: "Geometrical figures composed of various pieces of coloured marble and so disposed as to form labyrinths were frequently found in the pavements of French and Spanish Cathedrals. Certain prayers and devotions, doubtless accompanied the perambulation of their intricate mazes."[45] In later labyrinthine dances, the people held hands as they wound around. It is probable that the use of the labyrinth in the cathedrals was connected with chants and group participation.

A rare insight into the creative and spiritual use of the dance is found in the writing, *The Flowing Light of God*, by a German sister, Mechtild of Magdeburg, who died in a Cistercian Cloister in 1277. She tells how the soul puts on a white robe of chastity and goes to the forest. Here she feels inspired to create a holy dance and tries to "imitate the deeds of the prophets, the Virgin's chaste meekness, the virtues of Christ and His pious saints."[46] Youth appears, saying, "Maiden, thou hast danced holily, even as the saints." The soul answers: "I cannot dance unless thou leadest. If thou wouldst have me spring aloft, sing thou: and I will spring— into love, and from love to knowledge, and from knowledge to ecstasy, above all human sense." Youth responds: "Maiden, thy dance of praise is well performed."

A thirteenth century processional dance in which the clergy, choir, and people still participate is "Die Springende Heiligen" (the jumping saint) in honor of St. Willibrord at Echternach in Luxembourg. The people dance in lines four abreast up to the church and around the altar, singing carols. This occurs annually on the Tuesday in Whitsunweek. Ethel Urlin[47] suggests that this dance, which originated with the purpose of curing nervous diseases, had been practiced as early as the seventh century. Thousands of pilgrims from local areas and from other countries, walk in procession, holding sticks or kerchiefs which they wave rhythmically to help keep the group together in the step. Before reaching the church they begin to dance with a gliding motion to a traditional tune. The whole performance takes about four hours.

"The Dance of Death" or *Danse Macabre* was the most widely known of all the religious dances from the twelfth to the sixteenth century. It was danced in Italy, Spain, France, Germany, and England. Probably its origin was in the medieval sermons on death. The preaching of the Franciscans and Dominicans emphasized the terrors of death as a means of frightening sinners into repentance.[48] One early form of the dance was recorded by Cambrensis of the twelfth century.[49] The "Dance of Death" often started with a sermon on the certainty of death, delivered by a monk, usually in the cemetery or churchyard. Then from the charnel house would come a figure, or in some cases a group of figures, in the traditional attire of death which was a close fitting yellowish suit painted to resemble a skeleton.[50] Victims were then invited or coerced into accompanying Death beyond the grave. Death, although grotesque, appeared not as a destroyer but as a messenger summoning men to the world beyond.

During the period of the epidemic of the Black Death, between 1347–1373, there was less improvising in the "Dance of Death" and more of a set pattern evolved with musical accompaniment and a processional design. The whole of medieval society was represented from the Pope to the common laborer, and each man, regardless of station, was made an unwilling captive by Death. These people, arranged according to their rank, advanced in processional formation. Death indulged in grotesque and mocking dance positions. A small excerpt from a long poem on "The Dance of Death," which was written before 1480, suggests the type of lines Death said, when he addressed a minstrel who had come within his power:

> O thou minstral : that cannest so note and pipe
> Unto folkes : for to do plesaunce
> By the right hande anoon I shall thee gripe
> With these others : to go upon my daunce
> There is no scape; nowther avoydaunce
> On no side.[51]

Other lines from French manuscripts bring out the "democratic" mood of the dance, for all people were "equal" before Death:

> La Mort: *Saint-Père (Pope) c'est à vous à commencer la Danse.*
> *Je veux que le premier on vous voit avancer*
> . . . .
> La Mort: *Vous qui vivez joyeusement*
> *Ou jeune, ou vieux, vous danserez.*
> Le Roy: *Je n'ai point appris à danser . . .*
> *Votre danse est un peu trop sauvage*
> La Mort: *(au Fou): Ce que danserez, n'est en usage,*
> *Mais, pauvre sot, bein vous avient,*
> *Autant le fou comme le sage,*
> *Tout homme à danser il convient!*[52]

A peculiar variation of the "Dance of Death" arose in 1373. It was connected with wakes for the dead and seemed to have originated from a singing game of Slavonic origin in which the guests paired off to dance and sing. Then when a sudden shrill note came, the music stopped, and in the silence everyone stood still. A moment later when a sad melody was piped, one of the young men fell to the ground as if dead. The girls and women danced around him with mourning gestures as they sang a dirge. "Then one after another bent over the dead man and kissed him back to life till a general round-dance concluded the first half."[53] Again the death dance was repeated, with the variation that the boys and men mourned over a young girl. This dance bore witness to man's sense of mystery over death and his need to express it symbolically. Lincoln Kirstein says that this dance was used "as a magic cure for sickness" and it may be that people in the midst of the plague fell back upon this primitive expression as a release for their grief and fear.

"The Dance of Death" was known in Spain in 1360 as *La Danza General de la Meurte*. In Italy besides the traditional dance of death, we find a spectacular representation of death as the all-conquerer in the *Trionfo della Morte*. In Florence as late as 1559, there was a "Triumph of Death" procession with an oxen-drawn wagon upon which Death stood with his scythe and surrounded by coffins. The processional company sang the "Miserere." Baumker, in Herder's *Kirchen Lexikon* mentions seven French "Dances of Death," dating back to the fifteenth century, three to the sixteenth, and three to the seventeenth centuries. There were five "Dances of Death" known in England. John Lydgate, in the early part of the fifteenth century wrote "The Dance of Death." "Specimens of the dramatic *Dance of Death* have been preserved in the Altsfeld Passion Plays, in the French Morality entitled *Charité* and in the Neumarket Passion Play which opens with the triumph of Death."[54] There have been numerous illustrations of the "Dance of Death" on the enclosing walls of cemeteries or charnel houses, in mortuary chapels, and even in churches throughout Europe. One of the oldest pictures was painted in 1425 in the *Cimetière des Innocents* near Paris. Another famous one is "The Triumph of Death" in the cemetery of

Pisa, painted between 1450 and 1500. Holbein became interested in "The Dance of Death" and in 1538 made a series of drawings to illustrate the dance. Even today it has a hold on the imaginative mind, for in "The Green Table," danced by the Jooss Ballet, there is a modern *danse macabre* as Death dances on the battlefield sowing destruction.

Occasionally Christian dances had pagan origins, but became a traditional part of church festivals. One which originated in 1350 and is still danced today at Barjols in Provence is called the *Tripettes*, a patronal feast of St. Marcel. The Christian and the pagan merged originally when the people of Barjols, bringing the body of St. Marcel to their church, met a group of their fellow townsmen taking part in a traditional festival connected with the sacrificing of a bull. Even so, today, it combines both the roasting of a bull and several days of dancing in the church. As late as 1930 the program was reported[55] as follows: "Friday, compline and dance of the Tripettes in the church, followed by a farandole at the close; Saturday, High Mass, procession and dance of Tripettes around the statue of St. Marcel; Sunday, Mass, dance of the Tripettes, followed by a procession in the town with the bull on a flowered cart." After the bull is roasted, a feast follows. Here is a dance festival in which both the priest and the people participate.

An ecstatic dancing sect, the *Chorizantes*,[56] sprang up in Germany with a membership in the thousands, including both sexes. They would dance through the streets and in and out of churches until they were exhausted. They were not interested in the attention of spectators, but absorbed in their fantastic visions. For example, they might imagine that they were wading in a stream of blood, and in interpretative action, they would leap wildly in the air as if to get out of the blood. These dances first appeared during the festival of St. John the Baptist at midsummer in Aachen in 1374. They then spread to Cologne and Metz and other parts of Germany.

A similar display of ecstatic dancing occurred at Strasburg in 1419. Here St. Vitus was invoked to cure the malady. St. Vitus was a martyr under Diocletian in the eighth century. The tradition is that he cured the emperor's son of demonic possession; so he became the patron saint of nervous diseases and his dance was considered of curative value. Gradually the name of St. Vitus became connected with the disease known as "chorea."

The most ancient of the Christianized pagan dances were the fire dances which later became the dance of St. John's Day and the dance of "Brandons." The St. John's dance was celebrated on the eve of June 24 in Brittany, Provence, and England, and is still preserved in remote places. In this bonfire dance the celebrants leaped over or through the fire. It is suggested that perhaps this had an ancient health value because the smoke and flames tended to "destroy vermin and miasma."[57] The "Brandons," an ancient torch dance accompanied by chants and prayers, was performed on the first of May and at Pentecost. But Pentecost was also celebrated in a more devout way by the canons of Châlons-sur-Sâone[58] who had the custom of dancing *in prato* on the evening of Pentecost to the accompaniment of chants, beginning with, "Veni Sancte Spiritus." Nevertheless, this custom was abolished later by Bishop Cyrus de Thyard in 1624.

Through the centuries, councils were alert to curtail excesses in sacred dancing: Auxerre (573), Toledo (589), Châlons-sur-Sâone (639), Rome (826), Avignon (1209) and Paris (1212). The pagan element that was present and the undisciplined mass participation made it difficult for the consecrated and controlled religious dance to continue. We realize that the sacred dance had been overshadowed by the frenzied and grotesque "Dances of Death," the wild, exhausting dances of the *Chorizantes* and Flagellants, and the leaping torch dances. It was the coming of the Renaissance that brought balance and beauty back into the sacred dance and rescued it from its dark period.

The Renaissance (1400–1700)

The Renaissance is said to start with Dante (1265–1321) but he was ahead of the movement which developed in the early fifteenth century. In *The Divine Comedy*, Dante refers to dancing as the occupation of those in Paradise: " 'Hosanna! Lord God of Sabaoth!' . . . Thus, revolving to its own melody, that substance was seen by me to sing, and it and the others moved in their dance."[59] Again he describes the blessed ones as dancing in such various measures that some seemed to stand still and some to fly: "And as wheels within the fittings of clocks revolve, so that to him who gives heed the first seems quiet, and the last to fly, *so these carols, differently dancing,* swift and slow, made me rate their riches."[60]

This conception of heavenly dancing is similar to that of St. Bonaventura (*c.* 1260) as described in his chapter "Of the Joys of Paradise" in *Dieta Salutis:*[61] "In that celestial dance there is one who leadeth the whole dance, so doth the Christ (this sacred circling;) 'tis he who will be *leader of the dance, leading that company most blessed and preceding it.*" It was such vision of the highest in this art that became a guide for the creation of sacred dances during the Renaissance.

Elaborate and dramatic presentations were popular at this time and the dance was an integral part of most of them. Allegorical masques made use of symbolic dancing to heighten the dramatic moods. In England, to celebrate the return of Henry V after his victory at Agincourt in 1415, maidens danced with tambourines. As they sang and danced the people were reminded of David's triumph.[62] Another instance of the dance being used in a court celebration was in 1432 in London, in a pageant to honor Henry VI at the time of his coronation. In this pageant there were seven maidens representing the seven celestial virtues, and another seven representing the terrestrial virtues. At an appointed time "the entire choir of fourteen, clapping their hands and breaking into *tripudia* (dances) sang welcome hymns."[63]

Corpus Christi processions were originally nothing more than ambulatory dances in which the participants, following a certain pattern, bowed in measure, swung censers in cadence and threw flowers into the air.[64] In 1463, King René of Provence sponsored an elaborate Corpus Christi masque which was called "Lou Gué" and also "Jeux de la Fête-Dieu." It was presented as a series of scenes on pageant wagons. The dramatizations used no dialogue, only pantomime and dancing. One of the scenes showed the Jews dancing round the golden calf; another was of King Herod being persecuted by devils who were after his soul; at the end came Death with a scythe.[65]

That the dance is inspired from an inward, spiritual source was clear to Guglielmo Ebreo, a Jewish dancing master who wrote (*c.* 1480). "Dancing is an action, showing outwardly the spiritual movements which must agree with those measures and perfect concords of harmony, which, through our hearing and with earthly joy, descend into one's intellect, there to produce sweet movements which, being thus imprisoned, as it were, in defiance of nature, endeavor to escape and reveal themselves through movement. The art of dancing is for generous hearts that love it, for gentle spirits that have a heaven-sent inclination for it. It is a matter entirely different from and mortally inimical to the depraved mind which would turn it from a liberal art and virtuous science, into a vile, adulterous affair."[66] Here is a clear statement of the problem involved in the art of the dance: how it may develop as "a liberal art and a virtuous science" and not be allowed to become low or vulgar.

In the beautiful paintings of the Renaissance we catch glimpses of movement as the angels represent adoration. The flow of the costumes, the positions held for the moment, and the circular formations, all imply that the artist conceived of movement rather than static positions. The circling dance may have been connected with the "carols" of this period, for the term "carol" was "the name given by the *trouvères* to a dance in which the performers moved slowly in a circle, singing as they went."[67] Fra Angelico (1387–1455) painted "The Dance of the Redeemed" as a part of "The Last Judgment,"[68] portraying a circular dance of saints and angels entering Paradise. Ethel Urlin quotes a translation of a poem, "Il Ballo dei Angeli" as descriptive of this scene:

> Dance they in a ring in Heaven
> All the Blessed in that garden
> Where the love divine abideth
> Which is all a-glow with love
> In that ring dance all the Blessed
> In that ring dance all the Angels
> Go they before the Bridegroom
> Dance, all of them for love.
> In that court is joyfulness
> Of a love that's fathomless
> *All of them go to the dancing*
> *For the Saviour whom they love.*[69]

Botticelli (*c.* 1487) portrayed angels dancing joyously in a circle above the Nativity Scene. The composer of "In Dulci Jubilo" is said to have dreamed of angels dancing as they sang, and upon waking he wrote down the melody of the carol.

In Renée Foatelli's *The Religious Dances in Christianity*, there is a photograph of a sculptural work: "Danse d'eglise (Ronde sur ivoire)" of the fourteenth century. It shows a group of young women holding hands in a circling formation. Donatello's "Dance of the Angels" portrays angels in symbolic movement.[70] The artists of the Renaissance help us to understand the serenity and the adoration expressed in the sacred dances of their time.

In England, "The Franciscans let the people dance to Christian themes on village greens before the parish church. They made a circle, while the leader sang, joined hands around him, and came in with the recurring 'burden' of the story as he unfolded it."[71] Here in its simple form the religious dance served as a way of teaching people Christian ideas, and as a means of holding their attention on the leader. Again we recall the early "Hymn of Jesus" which had a similar design and purpose.

St. Theresa (*c.* 1555) danced at Carmel in holy joy. In the seventeenth century two other noted Carmelites imitated this Spanish saint: Bienheureuse Marie de l'Incarnation and second sister Anne de Jésus who danced before *le Saint Sacrement* at Carmel in Dijon.[72]

Although religious dances continued to flourish during the Renaissance, certain events occurred that were to have a crippling effect upon this art. Books began to be printed after 1455 and there was a growing emphasis upon the intellect with the printing of tracts, pamphlets, and books. The mind would soon be considered as all important and the body as valueless in religious growth. The Reformation which began about 1517 would tend in its most extreme forms to do away with most of the visual arts, leaving only the arts of printing, preaching, and music. It would soon abolish all dances and processions, except the funeral procession. The Council of Trent (1545–1563) which represented the Roman Catholic Counter Reformation, showed a determination to return to the liturgical tradition of the Middle Ages and so it removed many literary and dramatic interpolations.[73] In a record of the statutes of the Synod at Lyon in 1566 we find that priests and other persons were threatened with excommunication if they led dances in churches or cemeteries. The church was determined to stop religious dancing, but it continued in a variety of forms.

The Renaissance courts with the love of display often sponsored dances of a semi-religious nature. A stately dance, called the *pavane*, was usually performed at the time of the death of someone in the court circle, especially in the case of a young lady. In recent years, Ravel composed "A Pavane for a Dead Princess." William Dunbar in 1507 described a "Dance of the Seven Deadly Sins" at the Edinburgh Court on the day before Fastern's Eve as a combination of the dance of death with a morality masque.[74] At the Tuscan Court in 1507 Piero di Cosimo designed a macabre masque for the Duke of Florence.

When Catherine de Medici came to France she brought with her a taste for Italian dancing and she sponsored masked dances done to the accompaniment of psalms. In this connection Diane de Poitiers danced to the air of "De Profundis."[75] In 1572 Catherine de Medici produced an exciting dance-drama. It was called "The Defense of Paradise." The dramatic clash portrayed was between the Roman Catholic King of France, Charles IX, and his brothers, who were attempting to defend Heaven, and the Protestant King of Navarre and his friends, who were guarding Hell. The Knights, commanded by Navarre, attacked those defending Heaven. The fight, which had been planned in advance, left the victory to Charles IX, and his assailants were thrown back to Hell, which swallowed them. "After a long ballet, victors and vanquished joined each other in Paradise."[76]

Such a dance-drama must have been rehearsed many times. It is amazing to think that in this period when men were bitterly hostile, that the art of music and dancing could project, for a short while at least, an attitude of mutual respect and honor. How ironical this situation was—for the production of "The Defense of Paradise" was on the eighteenth of August, and ten days later came the massacre of St. Bartholomew's Day. So the artistic hope of reconciliation was lost. The conflict had become too bitter to be healed by the arts at this stage. Perhaps an earlier presentation, before the issues had become so violent, might have drawn the two groups into a common understanding.

A defense for religious dancing was written in 1588 by Thoinot Arbeau:[77] "For one who has spoken ill of dances, there are an infinity of others who have praised and esteemed them. The holy and royal prophet, David, danced before the Ark of the Lord. And as for the holy prophet, Moses, he was not angered to witness dancing, but grieved because it was performed round a Golden Calf, which was idolatry. In the early church there was a custom which has endured until our time to sing the hymns of our faith while dancing, and this may still be observed in some places." One such place was York Minster in England where up to the seventeenth century there was dancing in the nave on Shrove Tuesday.

In the first oratorio there was dancing as an integral part of it. This oratorio, *La Rappresentazione dell'anima e del corpo* by Emilio del Cavalieri, was performed in the Oratory of the Chiesa S. Maria in Vallicella in Rome in 1600. The principal characters were: Time, Life, the World, Pleasure, the Intellect, the Soul, the Body. The following stage directions were given:

"The verse beginning *Chiostri altissima e stellati* must be sung accompanied by stately and reverent steps. To these will succeed other grave steps and figures of a solemn character. During the *ritornelli* the four principal dancers will perform a ballet embellished with capers without singing. And thus, after each verse, the steps of the dance will always be varied, the four chief dancers sometimes using the *gagliarde*; sometimes the *cenario* and sometimes the *corrente* which will do well in the *ritornelli*."[78] Here we see the original oratorio made varied and dramatic by symbolic dances in the oratory. They served to emphasize the different moods somewhat like the contribution of the rhythmic choir in the Youth Pageant "Chain Reaction."[79] If occasional symbolic movement could be introduced into modern presentations of oratorios, it might help them to become alive for the average person.

A traditional Easter dance called the *Bergerette* was presented annually in the churches of the diocese of Besançon on the afternoon of Easter Day. In a book of rites[80] of the Church of Ste. Marie Magdaleine in 1582, there is a chapter on Easter Day which contains the following: "At the end of the sermon there are dances in the cloister or in the middle of the nave of the church if it is rainy weather. They are danced to certain airs contained in the processional chant books." In regard to the figure of the dance, there is this description: "The canons held hands in a ring, behind them was a second ring composed of choir boys, each paired with a canon, while in the centre was the chief dignitary, the senior in rank with the smallest chorister in attendance. After this, the circle broke up and the oldest and youngest led the way in a serpentine or labyrinthine dance." In spite of synodal diocesan decrees of 1585 and 1601 which threatened severe penalties against the enthusiasts who ventured to keep up the ancient custom, the dance continued in the churches of Besançon until 1738. By 1647 the dance had become less intricate, as is obvious from a description of that time which states that they all went to the cloisters where they held one another's hands, and then proceeded to make "three circuits round the cloisters."

The dance songs that were used had originated in the four-teenth century. They consisted of couplets, with repetitions arranged to suit the dance. G.R.S. Mead offers one in trans-lation from the Latin:

> Let the sober voice of the faithful sound
> Turn round and round, O Sion with joy;
> Let there be but one rejoicing of all
> Who have been redeemed by one only grace
> Turn round and about, O Sion with joy.

The notation of the manuscript[81] was in the usual form of the plain song:

si	si	la	sol	la	ut	ut	ut	ut	si	la	si
Con	vert	er	e	Si	on	in	gau	di	—	—	a.

The arrangement of the air, however, was in keeping with the *branle,* a courtly dance in which one couple leads the rest. For the research on this dance, we are indebted to G.R.S. Mead's article on "The Sacred Dance."[82] It gives us a glimpse into the music and patterns of movement that were used during the Renaissance.

The art of the dance was accepted as an integral part of all special ceremonies. Sir John Davies in his poem "Orchestra" wrote of this in 1622.[83]

> Stanza 77: Since when all ceremonius mysteries,
> All sacred orgies and religious rights,
> All pomps, and triumphs, and solemnities,
> All funerals, nuptials, and like publike sights,
> All parliaments of peace, and warlike fights
> All learned arts, and every great affaire
> A lively shape of Daancing seemes to beare.

Later in the poem he suggests there are many dance-dramas and that the directions are known for their presentation. Also he reveals that they are constantly creating new designs for these religious dances.

> Stanza 86: Thus they who first did found a common-weale,
> And they who first Religion did ordaine,
> By daancing first the peoples hearts did steale,
> Of whome we now a thousand tales doe faine,
> Yet doe we now their perfect rules retaine,
> And use them still in such devices new
> As in the world long since their withering grew.

Among the numerous religious dances created for special occasions in this period are the dance to celebrate the canonization of St. Ignatius Loyola in 1609, the *ballet ambulatoire* to celebrate the canonization of Cardinal Charles Borromée in 1610, and the "moral ballet" composed in 1634 to commemorate the birthday of the Cardinal of Savoy. Its subject was "Truth, the Enemy of Appearance, as Proved by Time."

The term "choir" meant an enclosed, elevated area in the church where symbolic movements were often portrayed. In 1682, Ménestrier,[84] a Jesuit in Paris, described the use of the "choir": "The divine office was made up of psalms, hymns and canticles for *the praises of God were recited, sung and danced*. . . . The place where these religious acts were performed in divine worship was called the choir, just as with the *chori* of the Greeks. In Latin, the prelates were called *praesules*,[85] for in the choir, at the divine office, they played the same part as the leader of the dances." Ménestrier goes on to explain that in early times the choir was separated from the altar, and raised up so as to form a stage which was enclosed by a breast-high screen. This type of choir can still be seen in the churches of S.S. Clement and Pancras at Rome.[86]

The grotesque type of religious dance also appeared at this time. One such was connected with a witch dance which brought about the burning to death of Jane Bordeau as a witch in 1626. The report was that she had been to a witch meeting and had danced in a circle back to back. In its design of following the leader, the Devil was the "ring-leader." The Devil's second-in-command was at the rear to prod the slow ones, for evidently the pace was important, "hence the origin of the phrase: 'Devil take the hindermost.' "[87]

A unique dance[88] was performed by priests at Eastertime in the cathedrals of Auxerre, Reims, Rouen, Sens, Narbonne and generally throughout France. The unusual feature of the dance was that it centered upon the tossing of a ball or *pilota*.[89] The plan of the dance was as follows: "When the *pilota* had been received from the canon or dean, the priests began to intone in antiphon the sequence appropriate to the Easter Festival: 'Praise to the Pascal Victim.' Then supporting the ball with his left hand, he began to dance in time with the rhythmical sounds of the chanted sequence, while the rest, holding hands, executed a choral dance round the labyrinth. Meanwhile the *pilota* was handed or thrown alternately by the dean to the dancers." "The passing of the ball backwards and forwards, in the circular dance, in which every dancer also revolved on his own axis, may well have been thought to illustrate the apparent path or dance of the sun in the heavens throughout the year and so of its 'passion.' . . . The ceremony at Auxerre was in closest connection with the death, burial and resurrection of the Christ —sun at Easter."[90] This symbolism of Christ as the Sun is mentioned by Lincoln Kirstein in reference to early church architecture: "The altar is east, for Christ is the Sun of Righteousness and rose in the Easter dawn."[91] So the dance at Auxerre includes a variety of symbolic patterns: the resurrection of the Christ—sun, the cosmic mystery of the heavenly bodies, and the labyrinthine dance.

Dance-carols were a part of the medieval and renaissance period. Some of the carols have survived beyond the period when active dancing accompanied them. As late as 1750 in Cornwall, there was a carol[92] which probably went back to the time of the medieval minstrels and troubadours. It seems to have a peculiar mixture of religious carol and folk song; for it tells the story of the life of Christ in ballad form, as if related by Jesus; but it has a secular type of refrain for a group response. Excerpts from the "Cornwall Carol"[93] are as follows:

> Tomorrow shall be my dancing day,
> I would my true love did so chance
> To see the legend of my play
> To call my true love to my dance.
> > Sing, oh, my love, oh, my love, my love, my love
> > This have I done for my true love.
> When was I born of a Virgin pure
> Of her I took fleshly substance;
> Then was I knit to man's nature
> To call my true love to my dance.
> > Sing, oh, my love, oh, my love, my love, my love
> > This have I done for my true love.

The ballad develops such incidents as the birth in the manger, the baptism, the temptations in the desert, the antagonism of the Jews, the betrayal by Judas:

> Before Pilate the Jews me brought
> When Barabbas had deliverance;
> They scourgèd me and set me at nought,
> Judged me to die to lead the dance.
> > Sing, oh, my love, oh, my love, my love, my love
> > This have I done for my true love.

After telling of the death on the cross and the descent into Hell, the ballad closes with:

Then up to Heaven I did ascend,
Where now I dwell in sure substance
On the right hand of God, that man
May come unto the general dance.
    Sing, oh, my love, oh, my love, my love, my love
    This have I done for my true love.

It is possible that as the church gradually closed its door to religious dances, remnants of them became parts of folk songs. The stanzas of the "Cornwall Carol" show an intelligent development of the life of Christ which must have had its origin in the church. Recently Gustav Holst composed his own setting to this carol.

Until the twentieth century a dance-carol, "Dance of the Child Jesus," was still held at La Roquebusanne near Brignoles. Little babies took part in it, especially those who were retarded in learning how to walk. After High Mass, on the day of the patronal feast of the church, the mothers with their babies formed a group around the altar of the Christ Child and one of them began to sing:

> Dance on the right foot,
> Dance on the left foot,
>   My good Jesus
> Dance on both feet.

She accompanied these words with appropriate steps and gestures, and each mother imitated her.[94]

There are two other carols reminiscent of dance movement. Both of these are connected with death. Ethel Urlin offers the following translation of a French Flanders folk song sung at the funeral of a young girl:

Up in heaven they dance today,
Alleluia,
The young maidens dance and play,
They sing as they dancing go,
Benedicamus Domino,
Alleluia, Alleluia.[95]

Closely related to this is a carol, "The Dance of the Virgins," that was sung by the lacemakers of Bailleul as late as 1840:

Tis for Rosalie they sing,
Alleluia,
She is done with sorrowing—
So we dance and we sing so,
Benedicamus Domino,
Alleluia, Alleluia.[95]

In these fragments of funeral dance-songs, we have preserved the ancient custom of using the dance to interpret the deep joy-in-sorrow which is a Christian attitude. These carols express the joy over the release of the soul and the acceptance of death because of faith in an immortal life of spiritual radiance. An Easter hymn by Palestrina (*c.* 1590) has a similar message. Here is joy in the *alleluias,* release because "the strife is o'er" and that "the song of triumph has begun." Exaltation is felt in the lines, "Let shouts of holy joy outburst, *Alleluia.*" Perhaps funeral services could have a more Christian character if, instead of mourning over the departed, there could be joyous acceptance of death as an onward step toward spiritual immortality. As Winfred Rhoades says: "*Alleluia* is the proper note for marking the progress of one who advances from this temporary abiding place."[97] The organist, Charles Widor, in his "Marche Funèbre et Chante

Seraphique" has expressed the sorrow-joy elements in death. If the funeral must be expressed somberly, let the angel song of spiritual bliss not be forgotten. The traditional antiphon following the "Mass for the Dead":

> In paradisum deducant te Angeli:
> In tuo adventu suscipiant te Martyres, . . .
> Chorus Angelorum te suscipiat . . .

has preserved the radiant Christian faith in the spiritual immortality of the soul as it is received into the joy of Paradise.

Post-Renaissance Period (1700–1900)

Although the religious dance had flourished in the Renaissance with portrayal in art, use in the oratorio, symbolic connection with hymns and psalms in services of worship, and creative use in allegorical ballets, there were at the same time, a number of influences that would soon close the door firmly on the sacred dance as permissible in either the Roman Catholic or Protestant churches.

The Roman Catholic Church had organized an administrative system with the central authority in Rome. This authority insisted upon liturgical unity with no creativity allowed in the sacred part of worship. So, with no growing edge for creative religious dancing, it either disappeared, survived in a few isolated places, changed into mere folk expressions at celebrations of weddings and wakes, or remained in a reminiscent way in the Mass itself.

Because the Mass has definite movements and postures for the participants, and especially for those who have the active service of transferring candles, books, censers, and other ritual articles, there is an effect of symbolic movement that is close to a disciplined, sacred dance. In fact, Hugh Benson, who became a Catholic priest, wrote of the Mass: "It is no less than a sacred dance."[98] Also, Father Malachy remarked in a recent drama, "But after all, Holy Mass is really a dance, isn't it? A beautiful dance upon the altar to Gregorian music."[99] Jacques Maritain, sensitive to the beauty of the disciplined movement in the Mass, writes: "There is nothing more beautiful than a High Mass, a dance before the Ark in slow motion."[100] *The Catholic Encyclopedic Dictionary*[101] has this statement concerning "Dancing": "Some of the movements of the ministers in sacred ceremonies (*e.g.*, celebrant, deacon and sub-deacon at High Mass) are in the nature of a formal dance."

By the eighteenth century religious dances were scarce. In Venice, during a procession of the Rosary, the dancers represented a triple rosary which moved around in harmonious designs. In Messine, another sacred procession was performed to celebrate the Assumption of the Virgin, in the seventeenth and eighteenth centuries. This included wagons with allegorical scenes in which there were choreographic interpretations. Jacques Cambry, a French archeologist, reported that he saw dancing in the chapel and in the cemetery near Brest in Brittany in 1766. In Liège, on the Tuesday of Pentecost, there was a choral dance performed in the cathedral of St. Lambert until 1794.[102]

The few surviving remnants of early religious dances which

have lasted into the twentieth century are to be found in Barjols in Provence, where the *Tripettes* is danced; in Seville, Spain, where the *Seises* dance in the chancel; in Echternach, Luxembourg, where the clergy, choir and people make a processional dance around the altar; in Russian Orthodox Churches where, during the "Cherubim Song," there is symbolic movement by the priests; and in the Greek Orthodox Churches, as a part of the wedding ceremony when the wedding party circles the altar slowly to the "Dance of Isaiah."

The Protestant Churches with their attention on the Reformation which had banished the arts of painting, sculpture, and drama from any functions connected with their churches, closed the door firmly on any manifestations of religious dancing. The Puritans went even farther, for they frowned on all drama and all dance as the sport of the devil. In general, Protestants felt that the portals of the spirit were to be entered with great seriousness through the mind and not through the senses. However, even in this strictness, some of the leaders were intellectually aware of the religious dances mentioned in the Old Testament. John Cotton, a New England Puritan, wrote: "Dancing I would not simply condemn, for I see two sorts of mixt dancing in use with God's people in the Old Testament; the one religious (Exodus 15:20,21), the other civil, tending to the praise of conquerors (I Samuel 18:6,7)." Increase Mather, another Puritan, condemned only dancing that aroused the passions in his discourse, "An Arrow against Profane and Promiscuous Dancing."[103] But, in general, all conventional Protestants came to assume that religious dancing might be done by "primitive savages" or "benighted pagans," but never, absolutely never, by Christians.

Aside from the influences of the Roman Catholic and Protestant churches, the nineteenth century culture was focused on the intellect and scientific investigation. In general, art was considered "of little practical value" and the dance (mostly ballet and court dances) was looked upon as light entertainment. People of that century felt that mental activity was so superior to any physical expression that the dance was relegated to the nonessential list and also to an even lower evaluation—that of being vulgar and primitive.

With no opportunity for creative life in conventional churches, the sacred dance faded out and became unknown to the church attendants. However, some sects and cults arose in this arid period and their members experimented with symbolic movements in their rituals.

One of these new cults was a sacred order called "The Free and Accepted Masons" which was organized in 1717. It grew out of a guild meeting of masons who were building English cathedrals. The moral code of the Masons was based on the symbols of the level, the compass, and the plumb, and they described God as the Great Architect of the Universe. In their secret society, as in other later societies, such as the International Order of Odd Fellows and the Grange, elaborate rituals have developed in connection with initiation ceremonies and the attaining of degrees. The members sit around the edge of the hall and leave the center for special marches and the execution of floor patterns of specific designs. The sister groups of the Masons and the IOOF also have elaborate formations that involve a great deal of practicing. Some of the designs which they form, in various secret orders, are a cross, a circle or more complicated symbolic representations of the sun, moon, or Pleiades. The members find a psychological value in taking part in the marches and formations, for it provides them with a bond of common action. Each one feels that he has a special place to fill. For many members, the secret order has a stronger hold than a church which usually asks its attendants merely to sit still and listen.

A unique sect which created intricate religious dances was that of the Shakers. They were founded in 1747 in England. As colonists they came to Niskeyuna, near Albany, New York, in 1780. They spread out through the east and the middle west and numbered about six thousand followers in 1850, but since then they have been decreasing until now there are only a few active communities composed mostly of elderly members. The Shakers welcomed all who were tired of "futile creeds, formal worship, and the evils of a corrupt society." Their beliefs were derived from certain Huguenot sects whose ideas descended from the Albigensian heresy of the thirteenth century. "There was an ancient tradition through this line for the use of dancing as a part of the adoration of God."[104] This fact sheds some light on their dance formations that resemble some of those of the early Christian church. In England, the early Shakers walked the floor while singing and swiftly passed and repassed each other "like clouds agitated by a mighty wind." The term "Shaker" came from the rapid up and down movement of the hands with the action mostly in the wrists. When they shook their hands with the palm turned down toward the floor, the symbolic motion meant that they were shaking out "all that is carnal." When the palms were turned upward as if to receive spiritual blessing, the quick up and down, shaking movement expressed the open petition: "Come, Life Eternal." Aside from this common motion of the hands, there were many pantomimic gestures to interpret their songs. General movements included bowing, bending, and a great deal of turning, for this motion symbolized turning away from evil and around toward good:

> I'll turn, turn, turn away from all evil
> And come, come, come into the gospel.

In the song, "Tis the Gift to Be Simple," which Aaron Copland wove into "Appalachian Spring," these movements are mentioned:

> When true simplicity is gain'd
> To bow and to bend, we shan't be a sham'd
> To turn, turn will be our delight
> Till by turning, turning we come round right.[105]

This emphasis on turning reminds us of the song in the "Bergerette" of 1742:

> Turn round and round, O Sion with joy (p. 126).

The first ordered dance of the Shakers was introduced by Father Joseph Meacham in 1787. It was the "Square Order Shuffle" patterned according to legend on his vision of angels dancing around the throne of God. In the Square Order Shuffle, which was called "a solemn exercise" there was a "forward and backward movement of ranks, the brethren and sisters in separate groups shuffling toward and away from each other, three paces each way, with a doublestep or 'tip-tap' at the turn."[106] In 1820 there was a variation of this in which men and women shuffled forward and backward in a series of parallel lines, weaving, in imaginative design, a fabric of union and love.

Circling dances were popular at this time. Sometimes there were alternate circles of men and women, as in Philo's description (p. 102) with the symbolism of Ezekiel's wheel in the middle of a wheel (Ek. 1:16). Walt Whitman witnessing a "wheel" dance about 1853 said that the singing in the center represented "the harmony and perfection to which all tend and there is God." By 1847 some of the patterns for their group dances were as follows: winding march, lively line, lively ring, square check, double square, moving square, cross and diamond, finished cross, square and compass. Sometimes they formed a "continuous ring" in the shape of the letter C moving in serpentine fashion. These group dances became traditional for the Shakers.

Always there was a growing edge of creativity afforded in the pantomimic gestures and rhythmic movements of "stand dances" done in place. Every created faculty, they contended, —the hands, the feet, the tongue, the whole body—should "express outwardly and assist the inward reverence of the soul."

> With ev'ry gift I will unite
> And join in sweet devotion:—
> To worship God is my delight,
> With hands and feet in motion.

Often there were "merry measures" done to a bounding, elastic step "to quicken the spiritual elements and to stir up zeal." Perhaps it was this type that George Meredith had seen among the English Shakers and described in "Jump to Glory, Jane:"[107]

> They jumped the question, jumped reply;
> And whether to insist, deny,
> Reprove, persuade, they jump in ranks

In 1850 the artist, Benson Lossing, wrote: "Their movements in the dance or march whether natural or studied are all graceful and appropriate; and as I gazed upon that congregation of four or five hundred worshippers marching and countermarching in perfect time, I felt that . . . the involuntary exclamation of even the hypercritical would be 'How Beautiful!' "[108]

Here was a dedicated group of Christians, industrious, creative, joyous, striving to build an ideal community and contributing rare religious dances. The Shakers welcomed Indians and Negroes, for their society was a genuine Christian democracy. Some of their songs were in Indian "pidgin English."

> Now see how spry me dance
> How nimble me can labor.
> Me will bow and me will turn
> And dat will mux old nature
> Den me hab de holy lub
> And dat be much de better. (1845)

The Shakers who had found a released expressiveness in their worship were hampered by an early ruling of the sect that there should be no marrying among believers. Also, they expected the second coming of Christ much as the first century Christians. So in their theocracy apart from the world, they failed to get their sect established in home-centered communities; and so their active contribution has lessened and will soon be at a close. However, these Shaker songs and dances are invaluable for use in informal work with present-day rhythmic choirs. Excellent research has been made by Edward Andrews in *The Gift to Be Simple* in the gathering of songs, music, pictures, and descriptions of "The Songs, Dances and Rituals of the American Shakers."

Negroes in American Christian Culture

In the early pioneer communities and even today in some isolated places, there have been religious meetings where along with revival songs spontaneous bursts of rhythmic movement have appeared. Although these were not religious dances, they were very close to such creations.

The Negroes who were brought to America in the eighteenth and nineteenth centuries welcomed Christianity, and as it became their religion they interpreted it creatively in spirituals and in rhythmic motion because they felt "moved by the spirit." Ted Shawn has written: "One reason I have a sympathy for the Negro revival meetings is that religion moves them so tremendously that they worship with the rhythmical movement of their whole bodies. Their feeling is genuine and they let go and are willing to express their religion." The "ring shout," one form of a circling religious dance, develops in this way: "The prayer of one man becomes a chant, the chant becomes a shout and the shout becomes movement. The spiritual, accompanied by hand clapping, becomes a shout, and the monotonous repetition of single phrases induces ecstatic trances in those who participate."[109]

The release that motion gives a person has been intuitive with the Negro. Even at the grave there has been rhythmic expression: "In 1879 the congregation of a Negro church in Arkansas danced for three nights round the grave of their dead pastor."[110] Sometimes in young people's groups in Negro churches, whether in New England or in the South, there are times of rhythmic portrayal of hymns or religious moods. In the group, one of its members may spontaneously start a pattern of movement and the others then imitate it and gradually increase the scope of the movement and the tempo. A Pentecostal type of spiritual joy and release is the result. In some Negro churches the members listen to the words of their preacher with a vibrant attention which leads them to respond with *Amen* and *Hallelujah*! as they sway back and forth. There is a contagion of sympathy and exaltation that the preacher finds in such a group.

The Twentieth Century
CHRISTIAN CHURCHES

The Roman Catholic Church is encouraging the Christian arts in the United States, in Europe, and in the mission field. Rhythmic interpretation is being taught in certain convents and schools. At Grailville, a School of the Apostolate for Catholic young women, in Loveland, Ohio, the students stud-

the symbolic interpretation of chants. In *The Catholic Art Quarterly* (vol. XII, Nos. 1 and 4), there are condensations of Renée Foatelli's book, *The Place of Religious Dances in Christianity*[111] translated from the French. Following the historical presentation, Renée Foatelli urges that mystery plays be "enriched with group movements in the manner of a ballet in order to emphasize certain parts of the play or to give them a new value. It would be interesting also to give a better understanding of the drama of the Mass by means of pageants which combine drama and dancing. These would be true visual aid for both the spectator and the participant. We could well take encouragement from the pageant-demonstrations of the Liturgy at Nimèque in Holland." Not only in Holland, but in London in 1933 *Everyman* was presented with a rhythmic chorus of Catholic youth, and in Berlin in 1933 there were 200 participating in symbolic choral interpretations of "Rorate" and "Adeste."

It is possible that the Roman Catholic schools and churches will welcome creative interpretations similar to Hilary Pepler's pantomime of *The Stations of the Cross*.[112] In discussing "Plays in Church"[113] Hilary Pepler suggests that the test of what is suitable for performance in church is whether it is primarily "a spectacle or an act of prayer." Surely the interpreting of Gregorian chants and hymns is an act of prayer and praise. Whether the art of the religious dance is accepted in the sanctuary or not, its spiritual value can be experienced in parish halls, in schools, and at outdoor services in the summer.

There has been the general policy in the Roman Catholic

Church to welcome the art forms and the artists of the country into which it goes for missionary work. Just as Chinese artists have contributed their skill in portraying Christ as a Chinese in their communities, so natives have been permitted to use their rhythmic ability to express Christian ideas. In the mission field of Soudain, Africa, seminarists have organized dances to celebrate the festivals of the church.[114]

Protestant missionaries are often faced with introducing a religion which has little symbolic, rhythmic design such as the native religion offers. Some make it very clear that the Christianity they reveal is purely a mental, philosophical religion with no movements for the worshiper, except to bow the head or to kneel. In South Africa, the natives have referred to one who has become Christian as "he who has given up dancing."[115] It is encouraging to know that some Protestant missionaries, even those who come from a conventional background, have been able to appreciate some of the native religious dances and to consecrate them by adapting them to the service of the Christian church. Recently, after visiting the South India churches, John Foster, Professor of Church History in Birmingham, England, wrote: "We saw dancing in the courtyard of the church. The religious dance is something carried over from pre-Christian days. The leader tells a Bible story, such as the deliverance from Egypt. The dancers form two concentric circles moving in opposite directions. Each dancer has a stick and as he passes each member of the other ring he taps his stick. Feet beat rhythmically, sticks tap to the same rhythm and through it all come the chanted words of the story with a refrain (like 'The Lord came down

:ions." "The Miracle in the Gorbals," a Sadler's Wells ballet, given in 1945, has the slums of Glasgow for its setting. It reveals the redeeming power of a spiritual person who goes among embittered and hopeless underprivileged people.

Kurt Jooss has made a great contribution in this social field. As the Jooss Ballet has stressed a more genuine expression in ballet technique, it has practically eliminated "toe" dancing. "The Green Table," to the music of T. A. Cohen, given first in Paris in 1932, deals with the struggle of humanity. This is a stinging commentary on Peace Conferences and the futility of wars, showing diplomats deciding the fate of mankind. War is not averted and there follows a modern *danse macabre*, as Death appears on the battlefield. As the war ends, the diplomats again assemble around the table in another conference of words.

Many of Jooss' ballets are genuinely concerned with human destiny. They are not an artificial escape from life as were most of the nineteenth century ballets.

Not only the leaders and choreographers of modern ballets, but also the dancers themselves are emerging from stereotyped movements and superficial emotional expression. John Martin commended the dancing of Nora Kaye in Antony Tudor's "Pillar of Fire," in May, 1949. He felt that in her use of the classic style she had succeeded in producing a profound effect. "The movements have acquired an inner justification that gives them emotional validity, as if they had sprung from her own intuitive responses. . . . There is a great calm, a great strength, that 'inner stillness' that marks the artist who has found his true dominion." In her classic approach, "there is in it no striving for effect, no playing for applause, . . . it is serene and noble. How beautiful the classic style can be when it has substance and awareness."

Although one often thinks of ballet dancers as competing for attention in the performance of their art, modern ballet groups are learning the deep experience of losing their personal identity as they portray great ideas or moods. In "Dark Elegies," a ballet by Antony Tudor, a father in sorrow over the sudden death of his two children, gradually lives through poetic-psychological experiences which bring him from bitter grief into acceptance of the tragedy. As a supporting background, there is a group of sorrowing people. Grace Roberts describes how " 'Dark Elegies' is taken very seriously by the dancers performing it. Consequently, one never sees a careless performance, every member of the cast uniting to convey the utmost in disciplined emotion. This is not a ballet in which personal expression or virtuosity is appropriate, and individual members of a cast of serious artists should not be singled out for commendation."[6]

Agnes de Mille not only chose a religious theme in "Obeah" or "Black Ritual," but she succeeded in using a group of Negro girls who caught the significance of their interpretation and radiated a spiritual quality which went beyond their technical ability. "Obeah" was produced by the Ballet Theatre in 1940 to Darius Milhaud's "La Création du Monde." George Amberg described it as "mature, beautiful, moving."[7] In writing of the dancers, he remarked, "There was a simple seriousness in the collective spirit of the group which carried the work emotionally beyond the limited technical capacities of the dancers."

The ballet has not been the best medium for religious expression because it has a tradition of spectacular display and stereotyped dance positions. It has lacked simplicity and genuineness. When Yvonne Chouteau danced Delibes' "Prayer," some of her movements were spiritually significant, but because it was given almost entirely on her toes there was an artificial atmosphere which counteracted the religious effect. The progress in the first fifty years of the twentieth century gives us reason to expect an increasing number of deeply moving ballets. The spectacular element may be an aid to dramatic power and its precise training may grow into a disciplined classic expression of inner conviction.

The Modern Dancers in the United States
ISADORA DUNCAN

The break from the traditional ballet and the start of the modern dance began with Isadora Duncan (1878–1927). She was the first dancer to react against the conventional ballet positions and costumes. She turned to the Greek dance with its free costume, bare feet, and natural movements. In her joyous enthusiasm she encouraged everyone to dance for his own delight. One of her theories was that "the body becomes transparent and is a medium for the mind and spirit." She felt that the movements of the dance should have a symbolic identification with the spiritual. "For the gymnast the movement and culture of the body are an end in themselves. For the dancer, they are the means of expression of the sentiments and thoughts of the soul."[8] In describing an experience she had while dancing to the music of *Parsifal,* she said, ". . . it seemed as if a spiritual entity quite apart from myself had been created as sound and gesture flowed up to the Infinite."[9] Although she hoped to "bring about a renaissance of religion by means of dancing," she did not have the disciplined life nor the link with religious groups to bring her dream to pass. Her protest against the intellectualism and moral preachments of the typical church which was ignoring beauty was searching: "Truth and Good without Beauty destroy the character of men and women." People with knowledge of science and moral law but without the experience of beauty have produced a distorted view of religion. The healing, the uniting power, the spiritual exaltation and the sensitivity that are in beauty have been lacking in our world. Isadora Duncan in her autobiography tells how the religious dance can be a "holy pursuit of highest beauty" and thus help all people to progress toward spiritual development.

ST. DENIS, SHAWN, LA MERI

Ruth St. Denis has been the leading pioneer in the art of the religious dance. Although Isadora Duncan had intimations as to the spiritual use of creative movement, it was Ruth St. Denis who was early drawn to interpret various religious faiths, and who has made a lifetime study of symbolic movements. Her interest in Oriental religions led her in 1904 to present her Hindu Temple dance, "Radha," which teaches that spiritual power and peace are attained only by renunciation. In 1939 she presented "The Masque of Mary," at the Riverside Church in New York. In 1931 she founded the Society of Spiritual Arts. This later developed into the Church of the Divine Dance which was established in Hollywood in 1947, and in which there is a rhythmic choir that takes part in the services and has a practice period each week. The purpose of the church is "to bring about a vital understanding between the church and the arts" and to provide a place to experiment with religious dance and symbolic gestures. A branch of the Church of the Divine Dance in Phoenix, Arizona, has Forest Thornberg as its leader. Its rhythmic choir has presented the legendary dance of the "Juggler" and has interpreted Malotte's "Lord's Prayer."

Among Ruth St. Denis' many religious dances are "Psalms 142 and 150" and the "Doxology." She has a "symbolic plastique" of "The Three Marys," and a dance called "Rhythms of the Resurrection." She has long cherished a vision for the dance that it might leave "the lowlands of mere aestheticism and entertainment for the clear austere summits of spiritual revelation." Ruth St. Denis has been creative herself and urges her students to be creative. In describing the religious dance, she says, "I mean a dimension of the free moving of our divine selfhood in any direction, in any posture, in any gesture or rhythm that releases our highest and most harmonious existence. The rhythms and sacred cultural forms may be Catholic or Protestant, symbolical or allegorical."

She has been able to find the spiritual truths in many of the world religions and to bring them symbolically through her art to American audiences. The world is her home and she sees God in it in His various manifestations through the religions of all races and cultures. Steadily, with great energy and yet with mystical serenity she has continued to discover more and more about body-soul expression. She has learned to dance joyously "the measures of the Eternal music."

Ted Shawn holds an historical position as dancer, choreographer, teacher, and enthusiast in religious expression. He was training for the Methodist ministry when he saw Ruth St. Denis and was struck by her art and its spiritual projection. The shift of his interest to dancing as a profession came during a severe illness while he was in college. Thus he describes his change of heart:

"During this enforced quiet I had time to think deeply. . . . And when I finally crystallized within my consciousness and came out with a form, it was the form of the dance as religious expression. . . . When I met Miss St. Denis, we found that our fundamental concept of the dance was the same. She, pursuing the dance upstream to its source, found there religion, and I pursuing religion upstream, found the dance was the first and finest means of religious expression."[10]

So, Ruth St. Denis and Ted Shawn came together to share their art and later in 1914 formed the Denishawn School which trained many of the dance leaders of today.

Ted Shawn decided to present Protestant worship in dance form. This was the start of church dancing in this country. In 1917 in San Francisco he presented an entire service in choreographic form before the congregation of the Interdenominational Church. The minister, Reverend Henry Frank, gave a brief explanation of the use of the dance in worship and then Ted Shawn danced the opening prayer, the "Doxology," a "Gloria," an anthem, a scripture reading (the Twenty-third Psalm), and a sermon which was a dramatic interpretation of the text: "Ye shall know the truth, and the truth shall make you free." The service was concluded with the dancing of the hymn, "Beulah Land," and a Benediction. It was a daring experiment, but it was well received by the critics and the large congregation. Soon afterwards Ted Shawn went on tour with his Dance Church Service in some thirty American cities, meeting with opposition in only two places.

In 1930 Mr. Shawn started his dance training center at Jacob's Pillow, near Lee, Massachusetts. At Jacob's Pillow there are classes in a variety of techniques from ballet to modern, in choreography, dance music and in the study of dances from all over the world. As Ted Shawn has said, "the dance is too great to be encompassed by any one system"; so the training at Jacob's Pillow helps to give the students a wide vision of dancing. There is a continuous flow, week after week, of guest dance artists from various ethnic or cultural groups who share their techniques and philosophies. Not only are international and interracial bonds strengthened by this sharing, but a deep experience of the basic religious nature of man is developed. In 1949 the students learned Mr. Shawn's dance, "The Evolution of Prayer," showing the development of prayer from primitive fear, through the stage of covenants, then mystical awareness and ending in vital, outgoing dedication. Mr. Shawn is a preacher in body, mind, and soul.

Throughout his professional career, Ted Shawn has promoted the idea of religious dancing. There are many references to it in his books, and he is glad to talk to ministers in conferences or in theological seminaries and to secretaries of YWCA's and YMCA's. At the Broadway Methodist Church in New York he preached from the text: "Praise Ye the Lord in the Dance."

In 1933 Ted Shawn organized the first company of men dancers with whom he gave many programs. Some of their religious dances were: "Nobody Knows de Troubles I've Seen"; "Invocation to the Thunderbird"; "Jesu, Joy of Man's Desiring"; "Revival Hymn"; "Battle Hymn of the Republic"; "Miriam, Sister of Moses"; "O Brother Sun and Sister Moon" (St. Francis); "Whirling Dervish"; "Dance That Heals"; "Job"; selections of *Passion of St. Matthew*.

"The Dreams of Jacob" was presented by Ted Shawn in 1949 at Jacob's Pillow. The familiar Bible story of Jacob becomes in this dance a life-history not alone of Jacob but of anyone who aspires to rise above mediocrity. In the first movement Jacob woos Rachel at the well, and Rachel is danced by Karoun Tootikian with the charm of the Far East. Then Jacob dreams of heavenly messengers who bring about his spiritual awakening and he experiences the prophetic revelation of his great destiny. As a part of Jacob's testing, he wrestles with the Dark Angel. The last movement is a hymn in which Jacob becomes Israel, the father of a great people. This work was commissioned by Mrs. Elizabeth Sprague Coolidge, and Darius Milhaud was asked to compose the music for it. Its stirring effect upon the observer is well described by Ruth St. Denis:

> These mighty gestures of strength
> Are symbols of the soul
> Revealing the vast ceaseless powers of man!

La Meri of New York City assisted Ruth St. Denis in establishing the Society of Spiritual Arts. She has been attracted to the Hindu dance and has felt its interrelationship with Christian ideas. Walter Terry, the dance critic of the *New York Herald Tribune,* has said that in her "Gesture Songs" La Meri has proved that "the Hindu dance, created and developed as a form of expressional devotion for a specific faith could express with equal verity and fervor the tenets reflected in such hymns as 'Holy, Holy, Holy'; 'Silent Night'; 'Eli, Eli,' and 'The Creation.'"

HUMPHREY, WEIDMAN

Doris Humphrey has a rare ability to present humanity in symphonic-like dance design. Winthrop Palmer characterized her as possessing "a grave and passionate search for truth, a faith in justice, an infinite pity for humankind." "My dance," she says, "is an art concerned with human values. It upholds only those which make for harmony." She feels "that compassion alone has sufficient power to civilize man." This concern and this compassion may come out of her religious background. Both of her grandfathers were Congregational ministers and she is a descendant of Elder Brewster and Ralph Waldo Emerson. Although her dances do not have religious titles, many of them have a religious undercurrent. "New Dance," for example, deals with social relationships, with the brotherhood of man, and with a vision of harmony in the world. "The Shakers" is based on an American religious theme: "God hath revealed that eternal life shall be the reward of the chosen few who are shaken clean of sin." The dance represents the Shaker sect at meeting and is a study of religious ecstasy and spiritual devotion.

"Inquest" is one of her compelling dances of social concern. Its theme is the accusation made by John Ruskin in a lecture: "You despise compassion." The action of the dance unfolds, as did Ruskin's story, around the report of a coroner's inquiry into the death by starvation of a wretched cobbler. A destitute family is revealed, the son begins to go blind, the father dies of starvation. Edwin Denby wrote of "Inquest," "we applaud it as a sincere and eloquent sermon. If a dancer feels like preaching he has as good a right to do it as any other citizen." Indeed this "sermon" has remained clearly in my mind over a period of years, whereas sermons which I heard preached in words in the same year have become completely blurred. Doris Humphrey has used her art for great purposes and with a radiant genuineness.

Charles Weidman and Doris Humphrey left the Denishawn group in 1925 and opened a school of dance in New York in 1927. They continued to teach in a number of colleges, as well as to create new dances for performances with their

Humphrey-Weidman Company. In 1947 Charles Weidman formed his own company of dancers.

Humor and wit have been characteristics of Charles Weidman. At the same time he has a serious message—that the power of a living art comes from willingness to project new ideas in new ways. He says, "The artist who attempts to escape the present either by delving into the past or in the future is running away from his 'center of being.' . . . Modernism in the dance requires that we, both artist and audience, be not blind to the life that surrounds us nor shut ourselves off from it. It calls on us to cease being static and self-satisfied; to be ready to say new things and to say them in new ways, and to make the dance a strong living art that touches us powerfully as we are today."

Among his dances, there is the "Happy Hypocrite" which ends with the transformation of Lord George Hell into Lord George Heaven. The Charles Weidman Company presented "David and Goliath" in 1947. A new and excellent work is "A House Divided," presented in 1949. The characters are Lincoln, His Voice, the Slave, the Lady, and the Stunned People. In this dance Lincoln speaks of the laborer, of the Negro and of a country divided. Through the vicarious contact with a great soul it provides a religious effect for the audience.

MARTHA GRAHAM

Martha Graham, who has been called the "Priestess of Intellectual Ballet," has been a strong leader in developing the modern dance in its discipline and in its intellectual and psychological projection. Leopold Stokowski refers to Martha Graham's lucid abstractions "where one can feel one's own mind pushing against the horizon of its limitations and expanding in a new and altogether stimulating manner." Martha Graham has said, "As we increasingly have something significant to say, we find more and more persons to dance for." So, because of her dances of deep significance, more and more serious-minded people are becoming interested in the modern dance for its value of revelation, rather than for entertainment alone.

It might be said that Martha Graham was one of the youngest church dancers, for at the age of two she surprised her mother by slipping out of the pew during a church service and dancing solemnly down the aisle to the offertory music. From 1919 to 1923 Martha Graham was with the Denishawn group. In 1926 she gave her first dance recital in New York as an independent choreographer. "The secret of her power," as John Martin suggests, "seems to lie in a tremendously disciplined inner intensity which projects itself with all the more force because it is so controlled. Her sole purpose in her art is to awaken and to intensify the 'awareness of life.' "[11] Characteristics of her dancing are humility, creativity, intensity, genuineness, discipline, intellectuality, and spirituality.

Martha Graham has a variety of dances that reflect religious awareness and radiate spiritual vision. An early work is "Vision of the Apocalypse" based on a theme and variations inspired by the Book of Revelation and the vision of a young monk. It revealed "the woes of man and the burden of his sins."

The variations deal with vision, toil, famine, blasphemy, ruthlessness, pestilence, mourning, prayer and death. Another early work is "Primitive Mysteries." Presented in three parts, (a) Hymn to the Virgin, (b) Crucifixion, (c) Hosannah, it portrays Christian symbolism as adapted by the Southwest Indian of North America. It reflects a blend of primitive simplicity and symbolic mysticism. "Chronicle" is a dramatic dance commentary on war and its destruction. "Panorama" presents both a depth and a wide horizon. The first part reveals Puritans in their hymn of dedication of a new world, and the last part projects the awakening social consciousness of the contemporary scene. "American Provincials" also deals with Puritan tradition. "American Document," with its dramatic unfolding of the development of our democracy has a "Puritan Episode" in which quotations are read from the sermons of Jonathan Edwards and from the "Song of Songs." Martha Graham stands out against the narrowness of the Puritan mind, although she reveals it with an understanding objectivity. "El Penitente" portrays the basic human problem of sin, penance, and salvation, drawing with profound sympathy and equally profound simplicity upon the ritual of the New Mexican sect of Penitentes. "Dark Meadow" provides an example of the overtones of spiritual awareness that are present in Martha Graham's dances. It is concerned with the adventure of seeking, and its various moods in this adventure are Remembrance of Ancestral Footsteps, Terror of Loss, Ceaselessness of Love, Recurring Ecstasy of the Flowering

Branch. The dancers are: She of the Ground, He who Summons, and One who Seeks.

"Appalachian Spring" is one of her most beautiful dances with religious moods constantly emerging. The program notes provide this description: "Part and parcel of our lives is that moment of Pennsylvania spring when there was a 'garden eastward in Eden.' Spring was celebrated by a man and a woman building a house with joy and love and prayer; by a revivalist and his followers in their expressions of exaltation; by a pioneering woman with her dreams of the Promised Land."

Certainly Martha Graham is carrying the spiritual vision of modern dance into new intellectual, poetic, and religious symbolism. In Roger's *Dance: A Basic Educational Tech-*

nique, she writes: "Historians say that the ultimate expression of dance, like those of every other art, becomes the worship of God; while philosophers remark that dancers who stop short of transcendence fail of their ideal destiny."

ERIKA THIMEY

Erika Thimey, who came from the Wigman School in Germany in 1931, has been contributing a great deal to religious dancing because of her sacred dances, her religious convictions, and her generous co-operation with untrained motion choirs of young people in over twenty-four churches. Starting with church groups in Chicago in 1932, in New York in 1933, in Boston in 1934, and in Washington, D.C., in 1941, she was supported by outstanding clergymen. Inspired by Miss Thimey's creative work in 1935 Dr. Douglas Horton asserted, "All the arts ought to be brought back into the church, including the interpretive religious dances, as instruments and mediums of worship."

Through the art of the dance, she has interpreted sermons, prayers, scripture readings, anthems, and offerings. She has a keen interest in presenting to church congregations messages of social concern dealing with labor and peace problems. In her programs she combines solo work with the motion choir of the church. Her group numbers are described in the following chapter.

In 1943 Erika Thimey established her dance studio, The Dance Theatre, in Washington, D.C. Along with her work as dancer and teacher, she continues to give programs in churches and colleges and at religious conferences. Since 1944 she has been teaching daily at Howard University in Washington.

Some of her religious solo dances are "Invocation," "Pietà," "Ludus de Anti Christo," "I Corinthians 13," and Whitman's "Who Art Thou, O Spirit of Man." The "Ludus de Anti Christo" which she first presented in 1942 was based on a medieval play of the thirteenth century which dealt with legends and prophecies regarding the Antichrist. The music background was selected from "The Planets" by Gustav Holst. The prologue was in the form of a procession and invocation. The three scenes were entitled "In the Beginning," "The Temptation and the Fall," "Intervention of Time." It closed with the epilogue in the form of a "Prayer for Absolution."

Miss Thimey's ability to pioneer in the development of the religious dance comes from her own conviction: "Because in dance the body is an expressive exterior of the soul, I knew that it would be possible to create worship through bodily form." One of her aims is "to unite the worshipers in a profound religious experience."

Her creative spirit leads her into a variety of dance expressions. Some of her compositions have a stylized religious quality as if she seemed to give animation to familiar figures of sacred painting and sculpture. This is particularly true in the "Pietà" in which the virgin yearns over the body of Christ, with the grief of hands and arms expressing their tender, bewildered acceptance of bereavement. When she interprets the inner struggle between man's benign and his negative spirit, she adds intense emotional and dramatic appeal. In most of her programs she presents some dance of inner or social conflict which strengthens a service of devotion in a Christian Church which acknowledges the struggle that is inherent in its ethical concerns.

LIL LEANDRE

Lil Leandre,[12] who has had excellent training and experience in both ballet and modern dance, has been active in the theater and in the teaching of dance. John Martin's opinion of her dance ability is suggested in these comments: "fluent technical skill . . . instinctive sense of form . . . extraordinary elevation." Within the last three years she has come in contact with religious leaders, mainly those connected with the "Camps Farthest Out." As she began to reveal her religious insights through the art of the dance, she found that her use of conventional dance technique was changing. She became interested in "structural body technique" involving posture, walking, and expressive movement. As she says, "I could only have created my spiritual dances from the knowledge and feeling of this particular way of moving." She has danced at the "Camps Farthest Out" in Redlands, California, in 1949 and in Bynden Woods, Pennsylvania, in 1949. Three spirituals that she interprets are: "I know the Lord has laid His hands on me," "Trampin', Trampin'," and "My soul is anchored to the Lord." Also she has created four dances to the accompaniment of the words of the Scriptures (without music): "Be still and know that I am God"; "Giving joy unto the

Lord with your voice as you walk in His ways"; "Follow me" and the "Twenty-third Psalm." "The religious dance," she says, "is a beautiful way to contact the dormant souls of men and women. As this new dance form develops, much that is now undreamed of will be manifested."

Other Modern Dancers and their Religious Numbers

There are innumerable religious contributions that are being presented constantly by modern dancers. Here are a few scattered references to some of their works. Hanya Holm's "In Quiet Space," "Parable," and "Trend" are marked by genuineness and inner strength.

José Limon's "Day on Earth" (Copland) is "an incomparable choreographic statement of faith in man" according to John Martin. Anna Sokolow's "Song of a Semite" deals reminiscently with the courage of several women of the Old Testament and ends with a march of new courage because of this tradition. Esther Junger's "Go Down Death," and Pearl Primus' "Sometimes I feel like a Motherless Child"; "Goin' to tell God all my Troubles" and "Great Gettin' up Mornin' '" have been deeply moving experiences. Eleanor King's "Two Characters of the Annunciation"; "Roads to Hell" and "Song for Heaven" are several of her religious numbers. Sophie Maslow's "Inheritance" brings a poignant, spiritual message to all who face tragedy but carry on with inner resources of courage. Jean Erdman reveals a visionary experience in "The Perilous Chapel" which is based on one of the adventures of the quest for the Holy Grail. In an article on "The Dance as

Non-Verbal Poetical Image"[13] Jean Erdman, the daughter of a Congregational minister, describes how the modern dancer gains "an immense amplification of spiritual experience" because the individual loses himself in this art. She continues, "Today when the cult of the self-defensive Ego, the self-expressive . . . individual has cut us all off from the unnamed immensity within us, dance again can serve as a mystery of transfiguration."

The art of the dance which was born in religion, but which went through a period of spiritual mediocrity, has achieved a new personal impact, a wide horizon and a philosophical depth. This art has a message for the people of this day because it speaks directly from the spirit of the dancer to the spirit of the observer. "If you come away from a modern dance performance as one who walks on air, chest lifted, head held high, a sense of renewal pervading your being, it is not because by sensory perception muscle has spoken to muscle, but because through controlled muscular action, spirit has spoken to spirit."[14]

CHAPTER XI

Christian Groups Using the Art of the Rhythmic Choir

Spontaneous Growth of This Art

CHRISTIAN groups all across the country are experimenting with the art of the rhythmic choir. Some are in colleges where skilled dance groups create excellent religious numbers for concert programs or vesper services. Other groups are in schools where children make up dances to express ideas or to interpret moods, many of which have religious bases. Summer campers, whether in youth conferences, "Camps Farthest Out," or recreation camps, find that the freedom and informality of these places provide encouraging surroundings for the use of the whole self in interpreting religious moods or thoughts. Rhythmic choirs and motion choirs are being formed in both large and small churches. Their members, drawn from the young people of the churches, work together to contribute their designs as aids to worship.

How does it happen that there is religious dancing in every section of our country? Certainly there has been no organization for sharing ideas on religious dances, nor has there been any promotion to develop this art. Yet groups everywhere are experimenting creatively! It seems that religious dances are springing up spontaneously partly because the "modern dance" offers an adequate art medium for the revealing of spiritual truth, and partly because religious leaders, earnestly seeking to make worship an act of consecration, are willing to try this art.

The modern dance has encouraged lay and group participation. In the teaching of Laban dance principles, Juana de Laban describes the value of dance-choirs. "The dance-choir becomes the perfect dance-form for all participants. The mass-action inspired by an idea, carries us to lofty heights where dancers and audience are fused in common exaltation. The joy produced by such dancing is enhanced in the group. An enthusiasm is awakened, like that produced by a symphonic orchestra, which holds thousands spell bound."[1] It has importance for the layman for "the movement choir is open to everyone." Just as a church is open to all who seek spiritual growth, so the dance-choir or rhythmic choir is open to all who wish to interpret religious ideas through the art of symbolic movement.

A spiritual frontier of faith exists in every church, college, school, and conference, and pioneers who explore the art of the rhythmic choir find that it penetrates into the religious experience of both individuals and groups.

Colleges

Colleges and universities that teach modern dance are building a valuable foundation for the religious dance in that the subjects of the modern dance include all phases of man's existence. So, in many colleges religious dances appear: "Ruth" at Bennington College, Vermont; Negro spirituals interpreted at Sweet Briar College, Virginia; a Christmas dance at North Texas State College, Texas; "Songs of our Faith" (using authentic music of the Protestant, Roman Catholic, and Jewish faiths) at Temple University, Pennsylvania; "The Creation" at Connecticut College for Women, Connecticut; "Our Lady's Juggler" in the Abby Memorial Church at Mount Holyoke College, Massachusetts; "Faith of our Fathers" at Otterbein College, Ohio; "The Sacred Dance as a Medium of Worship" at Howard University, Washington, D.C.

When a group in the Wesley Foundation in Denton, Texas, produced "Between Your Hands" in 1944, it was their "attempt to express in movement, speech and music the intellectual and emotional experiences of students who look at the world of their day with eyes that wish to see it as Jesus would have seen it, and who wish to relate themselves to it as He would have done."[2] The motion choir concluded the dramatization with symbolic movements of consecration.

Schools

Grailville, a School of the Apostolate for Catholic young women, gives a one- or two-year course which includes creative and devotional study and offers a course on the interpretive dance. Dom Ermin Vitry of St. Louis, editor of *Caecelia Music Magazine*, has given courses on the Chants of the Church and has encouraged symbolic interpretation. In 1948, the students created a dance-drama, "The Rhythmic Festival" on the vocations of womanhood). The next year they presented "Everyman" in which there was a rhythmic choir which interpreted psalms and songs ("Media vita" and "Attende Domine") in Gregorian Chant form. Here is a dedicated group creating interpretations of deep spiritual devotion with a discipline which radiates purity and holy joy.

Secular schools often provide creative art experiments in social, psychological, and religious interpretations. In St. Louis, Missouri, children of four schools presented "Man's Search for God," a sequence of dance and song. This was given at the Regional Conference of the American Association of School Administrators in 1949. Florence Fitch's book, *Man's Search for God*,[3] was a guide in some of the planning.

Socioreligious understanding grows out of this art form. Madeleine Dixon emphasizes the growth of tolerance that is deepened in children in her description of the creative dancing in the Oakdale Country Day School in Philadelphia in *The Power of the Dance*.[4] The children decided to study various religions of the city: Roman Catholic, Protestant, Quaker, Jewish. At first they spent time in considering the characteristics of each group. While working on the Roman Catholic interpretation, one of the girls, thinking of the nuns in their dance, said: "You can't just show how they feel. They seem quiet and peaceful, but you do not know what is going on inside. I think of the way they must look back on the world." So, as the interpretation developed, there was a solo dance of a young nun, looking back, with a chorus of gentle, admonishing nuns. After giving the dances, another child said, "The Quaker dance was like a fresh current of air in its simplicity, while the dance of the Jews had a vibrating tension." Miss Dixon reports: "The children dance all of the religious dances with a stark beauty of saying just a few things in each one. They speak with conviction."

Through imagining themselves in the persons of other faiths, their convictions have a stronger base for tolerant understanding than superimposed propaganda could accomplish. Miss Dixon prophesies that there will be a "lessening of bias toward so-called 'minority groups' in America through analysis and understanding of differences which children themselves experience in the dance art." When we see how secular schools reach children through an art of spiritual depth it makes us reconsider the superficial methods of most church schools—lectures or talks, dependence on leaflets, blanks to be filled in "work books," and such conventional, static approaches.

Youth Organizations

Girl Scouts, Y-Teens of the YWCA, and social settlement groups have found new and wider horizons of spiritual understanding through the medium of the modern dance under the skilled leadership of Ruth Uetz Noble. Using her training in dance, psychology, religion, and social service, Mrs. Noble has worked creatively with her husband who has been active in social settlement work in Chicago and is now director of the

Cleveland Chapter of the National Conference of Christians and Jews. She has created religious dances with Negro, Jewish, and mixed racial groups. Girl Scouts, Jewish and Christian, danced to the Hebrew "Haneros Halolu," "B'Roches" and to "Silent Night" and "Adeste Fideles."

"Dance is not just a form of pleasant entertainment," writes Ruth Noble, "but an art form that helps us feel and interpret life in its deepest aspects and helps us grow in our understanding of God and man. As we translate the poetry and music of people different from ourselves into dance form, we gain a greater insight into their problems and joys. One dances Negro Spirituals and Hebrew melodies and feels the wide range of emotions from despair to aspiration. One dances some of the great religious masterpieces and one feels reverence, peace of mind and soul, and a greater kinship with God. One dances the poems of Walt Whitman, Carl Sandburg, Langston Hughes, James Weldon Johnson, and feels the pulsating rhythm of nature, the strength and weakness of men, the democracy and all embracing love of God."

In our day which prays for peace, it is quite possible that increased participation in dances of racial and religious understanding may help in "the healing of the nations." As James Noble has written in "Modern Trilogy":

> When we dance together
> Then shall be peace.

Both the YWCA and the Girl Scout Movement have been actively interested in the music and dances of all racial and national groups. In the use of dance participation and rhyth-

mic interpretation, these groups find an approach that reache
deeply into the understanding of youth. The interest in Amer
ican Indians has been increased by the learning of India
dances by the youth in the YMCA (Friendly Indians) and
the Boy Scout Movement. These activities are paths toward
world brotherhood.

Summer Conferences

Summertime with its informal conferences and camps i
a re-creative time in American life. Because the leaders o
conferences and camps are enthusiastic over the use of proj
ects in which individuals may grow in mind, body, and soul
the art of the rhythmic choir has been welcomed. We have
already referred to the use of rhythmic choirs at large con
ferences such as the interdenominational one for North
American Youth and the International Congregationa
Council. In many state conference summer camps a projec
period is provided for a rhythmic choir along with drama
and music. At summer schools of Religious Education such
as those at Northfield, Massachusetts; Durham, New Hamp
shire and Star Island, New Hampshire, the curriculum offer
courses in the technique of the rhythmic or motion choir.

The creative work that grows out of the summer camps i
amazing. The campers are in a mood to re-create themselve
and to translate thought into body-soul language. The forma
classroom and the conventional church seem far away. With
grass under their feet, arching trees, beautiful sky above them

they experience the elemental feeling of closeness to the rhythm and mystery of their universe.

Adults enjoy the "rhythms" period of release and relaxation exercises at the "Camps Farthest Out." There are fourteen of these camps held in various parts of the country, and Alice Kraft of Philadelphia has led the "rhythms" for most of them since their start in 1935. It has been my privilege to lead this exercise period for a few years at the camp held at Star Island, near Portsmouth, New Hampshire. Each day the men and women join in simple stretching and relaxing exercises.

To take part in rhythms that have spiritual connotations may seem childish to some conventional souls—and I do not expect that everyone should feel at home in this art of rhythmic movement any more than one expects everyone to enjoy sculpture—but there is refreshment in becoming as a child to enter into many spiritual joys. As Christians, we need to feel free to use body-soul techniques to express prayer, awareness, joy, or dedication.

Rhythmic Choirs: The Earliest Experiment by William Norman Guthrie

When we turn to American church groups that have used the art of creative movement, we find the earliest experiment was sponsored between 1919–1938 by William Norman Guthrie, the Rector at St. Mark's-in-the-Bouwerie, an Episcopal Church in New York City. The rhythmic movements were called "Eurythmic Rituals" and used a combination of professional dancers and members of the congregation. About seven programs were given each year. "The Ritual Office and Dance of the Della Robbia Annunciation to the Blessed Virgin" was their first religious dance and was repeated as an annual event. The choreography was by Bird Larsen, a talented and spiritual professional dancer, and the music was Wolf Ferrari's "Vita Nuova." It had a disciplined dignity and graceful flow of movement. Although Bishop Manning attacked its presentation, the fact that he never saw it lessens the force of his negative feeling. In a letter to Bishop Manning Dr. Guthrie describes this "Eurythmic Ritual" before the Della Robbia Annunciation: "The lighting was so arranged as to give a sense of impersonality to the representation—one saw almost as in a dream. What followed did not resemble in the least a dance, but the performance of the Mass raised to an ideal perfection. . . . Here it was the Virgin who was glorified by assisting angels. The movements of the participants only faintly suggested flesh beneath the long white silken flowing robes, such as one receives from Fra Angelico angels moving in the fields of God."

William Norman Guthrie's keen interest in the arts of poetry and music supplied him with a wide field of subjects. His daughter, Phoebe Anna Guthrie, planned the choreography for most of the later numbers. One Dance Mystery he presented was "The Hymn of Jesus"[5] taken from the Acts of John (see pp. 98–99). The music was Gustav Holst's Cantata, "The Hymn of Jesus." At another time, "The Prophet" by Kahlil Gibran was portrayed in choreographic form. In its program Dr. Guthrie wrote this note: "Our friends and critics are invited to seek for the beauty of holiness or for the holiness of beauty, and bear witness that the age of creative, living devotion is not necessarily gone from the church." Other subjects were "Dante's Dream" and "The Vision and Gospel of Beauty" (based on the great odes of Keats). Dr. Guthrie's aesthetic mysticism made him a consecrated pioneer in the art of the religious dance.

Rhythmic Choirs During the Last Twenty Years

It was not long before leaders in various churches or religious groups—whether Roman Catholic, Episcopal, Methodist, Presbyterian, Baptist, Congregational, Unitarian, Latter Day Saints, YWCA's, or Unity groups—started to experiment in this art of the rhythmic choir or in the spiritual art of creative movement. Some of these groups have used occasional rhythmic interpretations as parts of special programs; others have formed rhythmic or motion choirs, to develop the art by continuing the training and experimentation over a consecutive period of years. That these groups have held together is mainly due to their leaders. Although there are an increasing number of leaders, four of them stand out because of their longer and more continuous work in this creative field.

ERIKA THIMEY

Erika Thimey though a busy, professional dancer, has been so enthusiastic over the spiritual possibilities of the sacred dance, that she has been willing to devote time to churches to train their young people, who rarely have had any dance technique, to present religious programs. With the young people of the First Unitarian Church in Chicago she gave, in 1932, a "Christmas Festival." In the spring the same group presented "The Easter Story" with an original interpretation. After an opening dance of traditional worship and a hymn of praise, a group of Light Figures gave a dance expressive of the search for light on the eternal questions of life. Soon there arose a struggle with darkness, culminating in a triumphal procession of Dark Figures. Amid the gloom of tragedy comes the illumination of spiritual truth. The new life within and consequent new contact with fellow human beings are joyfully expressed in a dance of renewed life.

Miss Thimey was invited to present a "Christmas Dance Service" at the Unitarian Church in Brooklyn, New York, in 1933. Arriving ten days in advance, she trained sixty of the young people to give this Service. At another time she presented a worship service with a rhythmic processional and prayer dance, using the young people in the Unitarian Church in Waltham, Massachusetts. She has helped greatly in merging the art of the modern dance with worship portrayed by young people, because she has ability, creativity, spirituality, and a co-operative spirit.

Rhythmic choirs will progress in the artistry of symbolic movement and design if more professional dancers like Erika Thimey are invited into the churches, providing, of course, that these dancers have spiritual sensitivity and reverence to guide their contributions.

ROBERT A. STORER

Rev. Robert A. Storer, pastor of the First Parish Church (Unitarian) in Dorchester, Massachusetts, wrote his B.D. thesis on "The Dance as Sacred Ritual" in 1937. In his church he has presented annually since 1937 "A Christmas Masque" in choreographic form. It is based on a processional design with angels who carry candles and shepherds who carry wreaths. His motion choirs have presented an interpretation of "The Lord's Prayer" by Malotte; a dance-drama to the anthem, "The Pharisee and the Publican"; "Easter Processional"; "United Nations Ritual" to music by Sibelius; and a dance-drama, "One God, One World." The latter includes an interpretation of the Jewish hymn "Yigdal"; a dance to "Now Let Every Tongue Adore Thee," by Bach; and a processional of color bearers representing the nations of the world. He also arranges special numbers for Children's Day, such as a "Flower Processional" (see Appendix I) and "A Gift Offering Dance." The motion choir has interpreted I Corinthians, 13 to the accompaniment of a speech choir and organ.

This minister has taken it upon himself to experiment directly with motion choirs. Working in a church where there is a tremendous, immovable center pulpit, he has developed a processional type of religious dance of dignity and beauty. Each week during the rehearsal time of the young people's choir he leads the group in a half hour of rhythms with symbolic motions, and then allows a period for improvisation. His pioneer work has a reverence that has made it acceptable to "conservative" New England. He has been asked to speak at meetings of the Organists' and Choir Directors' Guild in Boston. In 1949 he gave a two-hour lecture-demonstration at Old South Church in Boston as a part of a Lenten Institute sponsored by the Massachusetts Council of Churches.

MARGARET PALMER FISK

"Angels" in the Christmas pageant started the use of symbolic gestures in the South Shore Community Church in Chicago where I was a young minister's wife. Since the congregation was enthusiastic over the symbolic movement, the next year we had the "angels" do freer and more flowing movement. Two years later, in 1936, we had rhythmic choirs of high school and business girls. A special Lenten vesper service was planned in which they presented their interpretation of the tragedy of the Crucifixion to "He is Death Guilty" by Dubois; the sorrow of the three Marys to "When I Survey the Wondrous Cross" by Mason; and the joy of the resurrection to "Christ the Lord is Risen Today." At vesper services during 1937 and 1938 the rhythmic choirs presented "Jesu, Joy of Man's Desiring" by Bach, using a simplified adaptation of its choreography by Marian Van Tuyl of the University of Chicago (see Appendix II). They also developed a dance-drama, "The Prodigal Son" to music by Sibelius; "Sanctus" by Gounod; and "Hymn to the Unknown God" by Holst. Fortunately, the church was liberal and the young people enthusiastic. So the work of the rhythmic choir was accepted as a natural and beautiful part of special vesper services and pageants.

When my husband was called to the Church of Christ at Dartmouth College in Hanover, New Hampshire, I thought that its congregation would be shocked even to think of a rhythmic choir in a church sanctuary and so I decided not to mention this activity to anyone. But when the church women were planning a series of programs on "Religion and the Arts," it was my husband who suggested that I might give a program on "Religion and the Dance." And this group of liberal and open-minded women invited me to do this. Knowing that it would be an intellectual audience, I started my research on the history of religious dancing, which was the start of this book. After the program on the art of the religious dance, the women asked me to direct a Christmas program in which a group of fifteen young married and professional women took part. It was in 1942 that our first "Choir Festival" was presented and since then has been an annual event. The "Choir Festival" is a special vesper service in which the church's singing choir and the rhythmic choirs co-operate. Some of the anthems that the rhythmic choirs have interpreted are: "Alleluia, We Will Be Merry" by Praetorious-Marryott; "The Heavens Are Telling" by Haydn (a modern version of "The Cosmic Mystery"); "Agnus Dei" by Bizet; "Russian Easter Alleluia" by Gaul; "Cherubim Song" by Bortniansky. Occasionally a hymn has been portrayed: "O Sacred Head Now Wounded" by Bach; "My Faith Looks Up to Thee" by Mason; "Worship the Lord in the Beauty of Holiness" by Monsell; or a psalm such as Psalm 27 is visualized in symbolic movement. As a contrast to worship numbers, we have found that dance-dramas provide dynamic force; so we have created "The Perennial Problem of Job," "Naomi and Ruth," and "True Freedom," besides repeating "The Prodigal Son."

Wherever our rhythmic choir has presented programs

people have been universally appreciative, as if they had a great thirst for this art. This is true even of those who have come in a skeptical attitude. The encouragement of our church inspires the young people in the rhythmic choirs to contribute their spiritual interpretations to the best of their ability. Francis Squibb, a student at Dartmouth College, feeling that "such efforts should be encouraged" wrote in *The Dartmouth* concerning the rhythmic choir: "This group has brought a little bit of culture into an otherwise miserable period of world history. . . . Further, this work has done something to restore to the church some sort of meaningful ritual." But it is not

just Hanover that has welcomed and fostered the art of the rhythmic choir. Throughout the country many churches and religious gatherings ask for programs on "The Rhythmic Choir" and seek guidance as they form their own rhythmic choirs.

EVELYN HANDY BROADBENT

Evelyn Broadbent, a minister's wife in Easton, Connecticut, is active in the creation of religious dances. She has written a thesis on "The Use of the Dance in Religious Education,"[6] in which she presented the religious dance as of value in integrating the personal and social factors of religious living. She believed that she could apply her dance training to religious education projects. She gathered a group of fifteen high school freshmen girls who were interested in working with her to interpret religious ideas through the use of simplified modern dance technique. Her project was to show "the development of man's idea of God as exemplified by great men of the Bible." Saturday mornings were spent interpreting the material they had studied on the previous Sunday. They started with "And Man Became a Living Soul" to the choral reading of "The Creation" by James Weldon Johnson. This scene which portrayed man's gradual reaching upward, began in total darkness, then a dim light was slowly increased to silhouette the individuals. The second scene, "The Emancipation," portrayed the deliverance of Moses and the children of Israel. Elijah, Amos, Micah and Isaiah were presented through distinctive episodes. The closing number was a solo dance with a group in the background interpreting "The Lord's Prayer" to music by Malotte. In describing this dance, Evelyn Broadbent wrote: "The arms move upward in praise of the Creator. Sacrilegious to dance this sacred prayer? Not if you once see it done, or better still, participate in the experience yourself."

The members of the group will not forget this study because their entire beings were integrated into meaningful patterns of action. The direct impact of religious experience was felt by one who described how she had learned that religion could be interpreted by body-soul movement: "That's the way I feel about God—like in 'The Lord's Prayer'!" Another said, "I think 'The Lord's Prayer' impressed me most. It really put chills up and down my back." Considering that Evelyn Broadbent chose such difficult subjects—Old Testament characters and philosophic concepts—for high school girls to interpret, it is remarkable that she achieved such valuable results.

Since Evelyn Broadbent has been in Easton, she has gathered a small rhythmic choir of girls who meet on Saturday afternoons. Some of their interpretations are: "Psalm 23"; "Christ Lay in the Bonds of Death," by Bach; "How Beautiful are the Feet," by Handel; "The Magnificat"; "Ave Maria," by Arcadelt; "For All the Saints" as portrayed by the high school class under her leadership at the Northfield School of Religious Education in 1949. Rev. Charles Broadbent has commented: "In the light of our experiences in Easton we believe that under proper conditions, the dance can be not only 'acceptable' but beautiful and inspiring as a means of expressing feelings of adoration and praise."

Whether you observe or participate in the art of symbolic movement, you will sense that here is a revelation of the spirit of the Creator. This revelation may be experienced alone or "where two or three are gathered together" or in a large group. By using body-soul technique to train for abundant living, spiritual power comes to each one to glorify God and to serve Him with gladness. "I beseech you, therefore, by the mercies of God to present your bodies a living sacrifice, holy, acceptable to God, which is your spiritual service." Rom. 12:1.

Appendix

I

FLOWER PROCESSIONAL

Arranged by Robert Storer

Directions: Participants in one straight line at head of aisle.
Both hands held together in front slightly away from body
and about waist high. Flowers or green branches in both
hands. Group numbered off in 1's and 2's.
No. 1's start with left foot. No. 2's start with right foot.

Music: Hymn tune: "Llanfair" for Children's Sunday
"Worgan" for Easter
Both tunes found in *Hymns of the Spirit*

Steps:
1. All walk forward eight steps bringing both feet together
   on the eight count. This will take two measures of music.
2. No. 1's place left foot to the side, shifting weight of body
   to the left and bringing arms in half circle to the left for
   four counts and back to place four counts. Knees slightly
   bent for this.
   No. 2's do the same thing to the right side.
3. All walk forward again for eight counts.
4. No. 1's place foot to the side, bringing arms in a complete
   circle to the left and overhead and back to original place.
   Eight counts. No. 2's do the same thing to the right.
5. No. 1's walking forward eight counts bringing first left
   arm up straight, four counts, then right arm up, four
   counts.
   No. 2's do the same thing with right arm, then left arm.
6. Standing still, bring arms down to the sides in a complete
   circle, crossing hands down in front and back to original
   position. Eight counts.
7. No. 1's walk forward eight counts bringing left arm down,
   four counts, then right arm down, four counts, to waist
   high position.
   No. 2's do same thing starting with right arm.

189

8. Standing still. No. 1's step to left side with left foot, bringing left arm back and turning body so that you are facing the side. This takes eight counts. No. 2's do the same thing to the right side. Both arms are outstretched and feet slightly apart.

   This takes you through the music once. Go back to first line of music.

9. No. 1's bringing both hands together in front, step one step forward with left foot, four counts, and back to original position, four more counts. No. 2's do the same starting with right foot.

10. Bring arms to the center, four counts, and open up, four counts.

11. No. 1's walking in complete circle to the left and back to place, eight counts. No. 2's walking in complete circle to the right and back to place. This makes a pinwheel effect.

12. All bring arms together, four counts, and open up, four counts.

13. No. 1's walk to the left in half circle ending up facing front. No. 2's walk forward turning toward left shoulder. Both couples should be in pairs now. Do this in four counts. Then in couples walk forward, four counts.

14. Standing still, bring arms up on both sides, four counts, and down, four counts.

15. All walk forward, eight counts.

16. Standing still, bring arms up, four counts, hold them stationary for two counts. Bring them in to the center, one count, and out, one count.

They are now facing altar or pulpit table. Using a repeat on the music have them walk forward in pairs and put flowers on altar or have the first pair of girls stand facing front and take all the flowers and put them in vase after all girls have passed by.

II

"JESU, JOY OF MAN'S DESIRING" by Bach

Choreography by Marian Van Tuyl and
Orchesis of University of Chicago
Simplified by Margaret Fisk

Half of the rhythmic choir (ten or twelve participate) are the worshipers, who move only to the vocal parts; the other half, the circling group, moves only to the instrumental music between the vocal parts, weaving a pattern in a light running movement with hands joined.

There are eight vocal units in this Bach chorale and the worshipers move in these eight units as follows:

1. Walk in from a side entrance, attention on the worship center.
2. Come to the chancel steps and kneel on last note with heads bowed.
3. Reach up gradually toward a focal point, such as a cross, heads back, arms outstretched last, and then bow head as arms come down.
4. Rise and cross to the other side of the chancel, with eyes on the focal point.
5. Move forward diagonally toward back center with upstage arm raised, then lowered on last note.
6. Lift both arms high, heads back, progress to center back, reach up, then lower arms. (Kneel if worship center is not above the group.)
7. Turn and walk diagonally toward the original entrance for exit. Heads up and eyes on a farther focus, weight forward.
8. Exit with same pattern.

The circling group (or runners) acts as a balance in pattern to the "worshipers" group. The leader of the circling group is the key person always directing the chain of girls in the designs. Hands are joined except during 5 and 6. They move with a smooth running step.

There are eight instrumental interludes in which the runners form designs. The runners move with vocal units only in (5) and (6), as described above.

A. Runners enter before (1), weave in front of chancel, end center facing chancel steps. As worshipers enter on (1), runners raise arms slowly and lower them slowly.

B. Runners form circle back to back a little to side away from worshipers (2).

C. Runners weave about in a longer run, end in circle facing in. As worshipers raise their arms in (3), circle group raise their arms.

D. Runners make short run to opposite side ending in semicircle.

E. Following worshipers (4) design, runners weave a long run, end in compact group balancing the worshipers group.

F. Runners identify their movements with those of worshipers who are opposite them; move in design of (5) and (6) on the opposite side of the chancel, but gradually merge with worshipers at center back.

G. Runners join hands and form a semicircle, away from worshipers.

H. Runners form circle back to back.

I. Runners weave about in a long run and exeunt.

III

"THE LORD'S PRAYER" by Malotte

Choreography by Evelyn Handy Broadbent

This illustrates simple choral symbolic movement. The group stays in a wide semicircle behind the solo interpreter, in center.

Before Introduction girls enter and kneel together in a semicircle, with center girl a few steps in front.

(*Introduction*)	All fold hands in prayer and bow heads.
Our Father	Eyes are raised upward.
Which art in heaven	Center girl raises arms straight upward, separating them on the word "heaven."
Hallowed be Thy name	Center girl brings hands before her face, leaning backward until she sits on her heels. Then she bends forward in a low bow with her arms extended forward.
Thy kingdom come	Center girl rises to a straight kneeling position—arms are open wide with the desire to clasp humanity close.
Thy will be done	On the word "will" lift left knee so that by end of phrase center girl will be standing.

On earth	Center girl—eyes upward, arms downward
As it is in heaven	Girls in back, having dropped arms on "earth" rise to a standing position, eyes upward. Center girl circles arms upward and down.
Give us this day our daily bread	Cup hands in raised position as if to receive. Center girl only, takes three steps forward.
And forgive us our debts	Cross arms on breast—look upward.
As we forgive our debtors	Uncross arms to the side—look downward. Center girl takes two steps backward.
And lead us not into temptation	Girls in back take one step to the right, arms to the left as if pushing away. Center girl does the same, only crossing legs in four steps to the right.
But deliver us from evil	Arms move from left position to a strong reaching upward to the right.
For Thine	Arms stretched wide open, then back to original places.
Is the kingdom, and the power and the glory	Arms raised by degrees.
Forever	Arms circle down and cross in front upward.
Amen	Arms gradually lower until four counts after the music has completely stopped. Head is bowed.

References

CHAPTER II

DEEPEN YOUR RELIGION THROUGH THIS RE-CREATIVE ART

1. St. Bonaventura. *Dieta Salutis.*
2. *Training for the Life of the Spirit.* Harper & Brothers, 1941.
3. Graham, Martha. "A Modern Dancer's Primer for Action" in Rogers, Frederick M., *Dance: A Basic Educational Technique.*
4. Chin, Lily. "Liturgical Dancing in the Christian Church," Religious Education thesis at Andover Newton Theological Seminary, 1949.
5. Foatelli, Renée. *Les Danses Religieuses dans le Christianisme.* Spes, Paris, 1939.
6. H'Doubler, Margaret. *Dance: A Creative Art Experience.* F. S. Crofts and Co., 1940.

CHAPTER III

ENCOURAGE THE ART OF SYMBOLIC MOVEMENT

1. Coomaraswami, Anande. *The Mirror of Gesture.* Harvard University, 1917.
2. Oesterly, W. O. E. *The Sacred Dance.* The Macmillan Company, 1923.
3. Article on "Dancing" in A *Dictionary of Religion and Ethics,* edited by Shailer Mathews and Gerald B. Smith. The Macmillan Company, 1921.
4. See Chapter IX, pp. 133-134, 143-144.
5. Dickinson, Clarence. *Music in the History of the Western Church.* Charles Scribner's Sons, 1902.
6. Crawley, A. E. Article on "Processions and Dances" in Hasting's *Encyclopedia of Religion and Ethics.* Charles Scribner's Sons, 1908.
7. Ferm, Vergilius. *Encyclopedia of Religion.* Philosophical Library, 1945.
8. H'Doubler, Margaret. *Dance: A Creative Art Experience.* F. S. Crofts and Co., 1940.

9. Vogt, Von Ogden. *Art and Religion*. Beacon Press, 1948.
10. *Idem*.
11. Underhill, Evelyn. *Worship*. Harper & Brothers, 1937.
12. Delaumagne, M. L'Abbé. *Delsarte System of Oratory*. Edgar Werner, 1893.
13. Guardini, Romano. *Sacred Signs*. Sheed and Ward, 1937.
14. Sachs, Curt. *The World History of the Dance*. W. W. Norton, 1937.
15. H'Doubler, Margaret. *Dance: A Creative Art Experience*. F. S. Crofts and Co., 1940.
16. Foatelli, Renée. *Les Danses Religieuses dans le Christianisme*. Spes, Paris, 1939.
17. Eastman, Fred, Professor of Biography and Drama, Chicago Theological Seminary.

CHAPTER IV

START A RHYTHMIC CHOIR IN YOUR CHURCH

1. Ritter, Richard. *The Arts of the Church*. Pilgrim Press, 1947.
2. Maritain, Jacques. *Art and Scholasticism*. Charles Scribner's Sons, 1939.
3. Maritain, Jacques. *Art and Scholasticism*. Charles Scribner's Sons, 1933.
4. Duncan, Isadora. *My Life*. Garden City Publishing Co., 1927.
5. Magriel, Paul. *Chronicles of the American Dance*, chapter on "Martha Graham" by Robert Horan. Henry Holt and Company, 1948.
6. See Appendix.
7. Example of prostrate position:
   "All hail the power of Jesus' name,
   Let angels prostrate fall."
8. Fra Angelico fresco in the chapter house of St. Mark, in Florence.
9. Magriel, Paul. *Chronicles of the American Dance*. Henry Holt and Company, 1948.
10. See Arvey, Verna. *Choreographic Music*. E. P. Dutton, 1941.
11. Vogt, Von Ogden. *Art and Religion*. Beacon Press, 1948.
12. See Chapter VI for interpretations of some of these selections.
13. See Chapter X.
14. Andrews, Edward. *The Gift to Be Simple*. J. J. Augustin, New York, 1940.

CHAPTER V

LET THE CHILDREN ENJOY CREATIVITY

1. Ritter, Richard. *The Arts of the Church*. Pilgrim Press, 1947.
2. In *Primary Music and Worship*. Presbyterian Board of Christian Education, Philadelphia, 1930.
3. For suggestions on rhythms for children, see *Fundamentals of Rhythms and Dance*, by Betty Lynd Thompson. Barnes, 1933.
4. Diane Davis in article on "Children's Dance Theatre in Salt Lake City" in *Dance*, Dec. 1949, 503 West 33rd St., N. Y.

CHAPTER VI

BEGIN WITH PROCESSIONALS, PAGEANTS, AND WORSHIP
INTERPRETATIONS

1. Choreography by Evelyn Handy Broadbent, see Chapter XI, pp. 185-186.
2. Browning, Robert. "Fra Lippo Lippi."
3. Guthrie, William Norman. *Offices of Mystical Religion*. Century Company, 1927.

CHAPTER VII

DRAMATIZE RELIGIOUS IDEAS THROUGH THIS ART

1. Rogers, Frederick M. *Dance: A Basic Educational Technique.*
2. Article in *Motive*, Methodist Student Movement Magazine, April, 1948.

CHAPTER IX

THE HISTORY OF THIS ART IN THE CHRISTIAN CHURCH

1. Homm. in Lazar. i; m. i. 963 (Mead).
2. Int. II ep. ad Cor. xii; M. iii. 448 D (Mead).
3. Hipp. Ref. v.10, D and S. P. 174 (Mead).
4. Did. xi ii (Harnack pp. 444) (Mead).
5. Strom V. iv. 19 (Dind. iii. 17) (Mead).
6. De Prec. vii, 5 (K ii. 316) (Mead).
7. Hom. 1 ('In Ann. S. r. m') M x 1145, 48 A.D. (Mead).
8. Hom. ir ('De Christi Bapt.') M x 1334C (Mead).
9. Plotinus. *On the Good or the One*. En VI ix 8 (Mead).
10. Foatelli, Renée : "Les Danses Religieuses dans le Christianisme," Spes, Paris, 1939.

11. Ecc. Hist. II, xvii, 1 v 21 (Schwartz, II, 1, 140 ff.) (Mead).

12. D.V.C. xi. P 902 M. 484; Conybeare (Oxford, 1895, pp. 127 ff.) (Mead).

13. V.C. II xix (H. 49.3) (Mead).

14. In Eccles. Hom. vi. 4, M. i. 709c (Mead).

15. Or. V. (C. Jul' ii); M. 1.309 f. (Mead).

16. Vuillier, Gaston: *The History of Dancing*. London: Heinemann, 1898.

17. Ep. x i vi. 2; M. ir. 372—"Quid itaque beatus esse potent quam in terra tripudium Angelorum imitari?"

18. De Poenit. ii. 6; M. 508 (Mead).

19. Kirstein, Lincoln. *Dance*. G. P. Putnam's Sons, 1935.

20. *Ibid.*

21. In illud. vidi Dom. Hom. i. 1; M. vi. 1. 97 (Mead).

22. ib. 3; M. 101 (Mead).

23. Proem. in Pss. M. v. 532 f (Mead).

24. Homm. in Lazar. 1.; M. 1. 963 (Mead).

25. Foatelli, Renée. *Les Danses Religieuses dans le Christianisme*.

26. C. Ep. Parm. iii. 6; M. ix. 107 (Mead).

27. Ser. ccixv. 4; m.v. 2239 (Mead).

28. Graec. Affect. Cur iii ('De Ang.') Migne, iv, 8 9 2 B (Mead).

29. ib. xi. ('De Fine'); M. iv. 1121c (Mead).

30. In. Vis. Dan. iii. 57; M. ii. 1337 (Mead).

31. Int. Jonae Proph. Arg.; M. ii. 1721 (Mead).

32. Glück, Heinrich. *Die Christliche Kunst des Ostens*, Berlin, 1923. Plate 11.

33. Phillips, William. *Carols*. E. P. Dutton, 1921.

34. Kinney, Troy. *Dance*. Frederick A. Stokes Co., 1914.

35. Phillips, William. *Carols*.

36. Perugini, Mark. *The Pageant of the Dance Ballet*. Jarrolds, London, 1946.

37. *Ibid.*

38. *Planctus* of Cividale del Fruili. Cividale, Reale Museo Archelogico, M Sc J, Process. Cividalenso Saec. xiv, foll 74-76.

39. Kirstein, Lincoln. *Dance*. G. P. Putnam's Sons, 1935.

40. Foatelli, Renée. *Les Danses Religieuses dans le Christianisme*.

41. Arvey, Verna. *Choreographic Music*. E. P. Dutton, 1941.

42. Journal of Eudes Rigaud, Archbishop of Rouen (1275) (Foatelli).

43. Foatelli, Renée. *Les Danses Religieuses dans le Christianisme*.

44. Mead. "The Sacred Dance."

45. Poole, T. H. "Labyrinth" in *The Catholic Encyclopedia*. London, 1910.

46. Kirstein, Lincoln. *Dance*. G. P. Putnam's Sons, 1935.

47. Urlin, Ethel. *Dancing, Ancient and Modern*. Appleton & Co., 1914.

48. Warren, Florence. *The Dance of Death*. Oxford University Press, 1931.

49. Sachs, Kurt. *World History of the Dance*. W. W. Norton., 1937.

50. Herbermann, Charles. "The Dance of Death" in *The Catholic Encyclopedia*.

51. Warren, Florence. *The Dance of Death*. Oxford University Press, 1931.

52. Foatelli, Renée. *Les Danses Religieuses dans le Christianisme*.

53. Kirstein, Lincoln. *Dance*. G. P. Putnam's Sons, 1935.

54. Herbermann, Charles. "The Dance of Death" in *The Catholic Encyclopedia*.

55. Article by M. E. Dermenghem, in *Le Correspondant*, May, 1936 (Foatelli).

56. Haück, A. "Chorizantes." New Schaff-Herzog *Encyclopedia of Religious Knowledge*.

57. Foatelli, Renée. *Les Danses Religieuses dans le Christianisme*.

58. Dom Martène. *Danses d'Eglise au Moyen Age* (395-1453) (Foatelli).

59. Dante. *Divine Comedy*, Paradise VII: 1-6. Houghton Mifflin, 1920.

60. *Ibid.* Paradise XXIV: 11-15.

61. *Dieta Salutis* in Cap. 1. "Aureus Libellus" printed in 1518 in Venice.

62. Kirstein, Lincoln. *Dance*. G. P. Putnam's Sons, 1935.

63. *Ibid.*

64. Foatelli, Renée. *Les Danses Religieuses dans le Christianisme*.

65. Kinney, Troy. *Dance*. Frederick A. Stokes Co., and Vuillier, Gaston. *The History of the Dance*. London: Heinemann, 1898.

66. Kinkeldy, Otto. "A Jewish Dancing Master of the Renaissance: Gugliemo Ebres" in A. S. Friendus Memorial Volume.

67. Urlin, Ethel. *Dancing, Ancient and Modern*. Appleton & Co., 1914.

68. "The Last Judgment" in the Monastery of St. Mark in Florence.

69. Urlin, Ethel. *Dancing, Ancient and Modern*. Appleton & Co., 1914.

70. In the museum of Santa Maria dei Fiore in Florence.

71. Foster, John. *Then and Now*, Harper & Brothers, 1942.

72. Foatelli, Renée. *Les Danses Religieuses dans le Christianisme.*
73. Young, Karl. *The Drama of the Medieval Church.* Clarendon Press, 1933.
74. Kirstein, Lincoln. *Dance.* G. P. Putnam's Sons, 1935.
75. Arvey, Verna. *Choreographic Music.* E. P. Dutton, 1941.
76. Kirstein, Lincoln. *Dance.* G. P. Putnam's Sons, 1935.
77. Arbeau, Thoinot (Jehan Tabouret). *Orchesography.* London: Beaumont, 1925.
78. *Grove's Dictionary of Music and Musicians,* ed. by H. C. Colles. London: The Macmillan Company.
79. See Chapter VII, pp. 91-92.
80. Rites referred to in an anonymous "Letter to the *Mercure de France*" of September, 1742. *Op. cit.* pp. 1930 ff. (Mead).
81. Ms. presented to the cathedral by a canon named Hugh de Vilète of Besançon at the beginning of the fifteenth century (Mead).
82. Mead, G. R. S. *The Sacred Dance.*
83. Davies, John. "Orchestra: or a Poem expressing the Antiquitie of Dancing." (Printed by A.M. for Richard Hawkins, London, 1622).
84. Ménestrier. *Des Ballet Anciens et Modernes.* Paris, 1682.
85. The priests of ancient Roman dancing guild of the Salii were called praesules because they led the dance in public (Mead).
86. Mead, G.R.S. "The Sacred Dance" in Quest Reprint Series No. 11. London: Watkins, 1926.
87. Avebury, John. *The Origins of Civilization.* Longmans, Green, 1912.
88. An account by Abbé LeBeuf in a letter to the *Mercure de France* of May, 1726, concerning a Latin Ms. of the Cathedral of Auxerre (Mead).
89. "Pilota"—a little larger than a tennis ball; referred to as early as 1398 (Mead).
90. Mead, G.R.S. "The Sacred Dance," pp. 109, 110.
91. Kirstein, Lincoln. *Dance.* G. P. Putnam's Sons, 1935.
92. "Cornwall Carol," recorded by William Sandys in *Christmas Carols, Ancient and Modern,* London, 1833 (Mead).
93. "Cornwall Carol," music by Gustav Holst: "This Have I Done for my True Love."
94. Foatelli, Renée. *Les Danses Religieuses dans le Christianisme.*
95. Urlin, Ethel. *Dancing, Ancient and Modern.* Appleton & Co., 1914. p. 48.
96. *Ibid.,* p. 49.

97. Rhoades, Winfred. "When Grief Stabs the Heart." *Advance*, N. Y. Aug. 1949.

98. Benson, Hugh. *Papers of a Pariah.*

99. Doherty, Brian. *Father Malachy's Miracle.* Random House, 1938.

100. Maritain, Jacques. *Art and Scholasticism.* Charles Scribner's Sons, 1933.

101. *The Catholic Encyclopedic Dictionary.* The Macmillan Company, 1931.

102. Foatelli, Renée. *Les Danses Religieuses dans le Christianisme.*

103. Published in 1688 by The Ministers of Christ at Boston in New England.

104. Andrews, E. D. "The Dance in Shaker Ritual" in Magriel, Paul. *Chronicles of the American Dance.* Henry Holt and Company, 1948.

105. Andrews, E. D. *The Gift to Be Simple: Songs, Dances and Rituals of the American Shakers.* (All of the songs included in this section on the Shakers are taken from this book.)

106. Andrews, E. D. "The Dance in Shaker Ritual" in Magriel's *Chronicles of the American Dance.* Henry Holt and Company, 1948.

107. Meredith, George. *Poems.* Charles Scribner's Sons, 1905 (p. 414).

108. Andrews, E. D. "The Dance in Shaker Ritual" (Magriel).

109. Arvey, Verna. *Choreographic Music.* E. P. Dutton & Co., 1941.

110. *Encyclopedia of Religion and Ethics.*

111. Foatelli, Renée. *Les Danses Religieuses dans le Christianisme.*

112. "The Stations of the Cross" as devised for liturgical presentation by H. D. C. Pepler, Blackfriars, Oxford, 1933.

113. Pepler, Hilary. "Plays in Church" in *The Catholic Art Quarterly* (vol. XII, No. 4).

114. Foatelli, Renée. *Les Danses Religieuses dans le Christianisme.*

115. Fritsch. *Die Einzeborenen Sud-Africa's,* 1872. Referred to in Oesterly. *The Sacred Dance.* The Macmillan Company, 1923.

116. Foster, John. *Then and Now.* Harper & Brothers, 1942.

117. *Pilgrim Youth,* 14 Beacon St., Boston, Mass.

CHAPTER X

PROFESSIONAL ARTISTS CHOOSE RELIGIOUS THEMES

1. Palmer, Winthrop. *Theatrical Dancing in America.* Bernard Ackerman, 1945.

2. Amberg, George. *Art in Modern Ballet.* Pantheon Books, 1946.

3. Kinney, Troy. *The Dance*. Frederick A. Stokes Co., 1914.
4. Denby, Edwin. *Looking at the Dance*. Pellegrini & Cudahy, 1949.
5. Roberts, Grace. *The Borzoi Book of Ballets*. Alfred A. Knopf, 1946.
6. *Ibid*.
7. Amberg, George. *Ballet*, a Mentor book. The New American Library, N. Y., 1949.
8. Palmer, Winthrop. *Theatrical Dancing in America*. Bernard Ackerman, 1945.
9. Duncan, Isadora. *My Life*. Garden City Publishing Co., 1927.
10. Shawn, Ted. *The American Ballet*. Henry Holt and Company, N. Y., 1926.
11. *New York Times*, May 7, 1944.
12. Lil Leandre, of Santa Fe, New Mexico.
13. *Dance Observer*, 55 W. 11th St., New York, N. Y., May, 1949.
14. Lloyd, Margaret. *The Borzoi Book of Modern Dance*. Alfred A. Knopf, N. Y., 1929.

CHAPTER XI

CHRISTIAN GROUPS USING THE ART OF THE RHYTHMIC CHOIR

1. Rogers, Frederick. *Dance: A Basic Educational Technique*. The Macmillan Company, 1941.
2. *Motive*, February, 1942, Nashville, Tenn.
3. Fitch, Florence. *Man's Search for God*.
4. Dixon, Madeleine. *The Power of the Dance*. John Day Company, 1939.
5. Office to Von Holst's Cantata in *Offices of Mystical Religion*. Century Company, 1927.
6. Broadbent, Evelyn. "The Use of the Dance in Religious Education," Master's Thesis at Chicago Theological Seminary, 1943.

Bibliography

Andrews, E. D. *The Gift to Be Simple*. J. J. Augustin, N. Y., 1940.

Apochryphal New Testament. Clarendon Press, Oxford, 1945.

Arbeau, Thoinot. *Orchesography*. London: Beaumont, 1925.

Amberg, George. *Art in Modern Ballet*. Pantheon Books, 1946.

Armitage, Merle. *Dance Memories*. Duell, Sloan and Pierce, 1947.

Arvey, Verna. *Choreographic Music*. E. P. Dutton & Co., 1941.

Avebury, John. *The Origins of Civilization*. Longmans, Green & Co., 1912.

Benson, Hugh. *Papers of a Pariah*. Longmans, Green & Co., 1907.

Carpenter, Edward. *Pagan and Christian Creeds*. Harcourt, Brace, 1920.

Catholic Encyclopedia, Vol. IV. Encyclopedia Press, 1913.

Catholic Encyclopedic Dictionary. The Macmillan Company, 1931.

Dante Alighieri. *The Divine Comedy*. Houghton, Mifflin Co., 1920.

Delaumagne, M. L'Abbé. *Delsarte System of Oratory*. Werner, 1893.

Denby, Edwin. *Looking at the Dance*. Pellegrini & Cudahy, 1949.

Dickinson, Edward. *Music in the History of the Western Church*. Charles Scribner's Sons, 1902.

Dictionary of Religion and Ethics, ed. by Shailer Mathews and Gerald Smith. The Macmillan Company, 1921.

Dixon, Madeleine. *The Power of the Dance*. John Day Company, 1939.

Duncan, Isadora. *My Life*. Garden City Publishing Co., 1927.

Eastman, Fred. *Modern Religious Dramas*. Henry Holt and Company, 1928.

Ellis, Havelock. *The Dance of Life*. Houghton, Mifflin Co., 1923.

Ferm, Vergilius. *Encyclopedia of Religion*. Philosophical Library, 1945.

Foatelli, Renée. *Les Danses Religieuses dans le Christianisme*. Spes, Paris, 1939.

Foster, John. *Then and Now*. Harper & Brothers, 1942.

Grove's Dictionary of Music and Musicians, ed. by H. C. Colles. London: The Macmillan Company, 1928.

Guthrie, William Norman. *Offices of Mystical Religion*. Century Company, 1927.

Hambly, Wilfred. *Tribal Dancing and Social Development*. London, 1926.

Hastings, James. *Encyclopedia of Religion and Ethics*. Charles Scribner's Sons, 1908.

H'Doubler, Margaret. *Dance: A Creative Art Experience*. F. S. Crofts and Co., 1940.

Kinney, Troy. *The Dance*. Frederick A. Stokes Co., 1914.

Kirstein, Lincoln. *Dance*. G. P. Putnam's Sons, 1935.

La Meri. *The Gesture Language of the Hindu Dance*. Columbia University, 1941.

Magriel, Paul. *Chronicles of the American Dance*. Henry Holt and Company, 1948.

Maritain, Jacques. *Art and Scholasticism*. Charles Scribner's Sons, 1933.

Martin, John. *America Dancing*. Dodge Publishing Co., 1936.

—— *Introduction to the Dance*. W. W. Norton & Co., 1939.

Mason, Bernard. *Dances and Stories of the American Indian*. Barnes, 1944.

Mead, G. R. S. "The Sacred Dance in Christendom" in *The Quest: A Quarterly Review*, Quest Reprint Series, No. 11, Watkins, London, 1926.

Morgan, Barbara. *Martha Graham*. Duell, Sloan & Pierce, 1941.

New Schaff-Herzog *Encyclopedia of Religion*. Funk & Wagnalls, 1909.

Oesterly, W. O. E. *The Sacred Dance*. The Macmillan Company, 1923.

Palmer, Winthrop. *Theatrical Dancing in America*. Bernard Ackerman, 1945.

Perugini, Mark. *A Pageant of the Dance Ballet*. Jarrolds, London, 1946.

Phillips, William. *Carols*. E. P. Dutton, 1921.

Ritter, Richard. *The Arts of the Church*. Pilgrim Press, 1947.

Rogers, Frederick. *Dance: A Basic Educational Technique*. The Macmillan Company, 1941.

Sachs, Curt. *The World History of the Dance*. W. W. Norton, 1937.

Selden, Elizabeth. *The Dancer's Quest*. Univ. of California Press, 1935.

Shawn, Ted. *The American Ballet*. Henry Holt and Company, 1926.

—— *Dance We Must*. Eagle Printing & Binding Co., 1940.

—— *Gods Who Dance*. E. P. Dutton, 1929.

St. Denis, Ruth. *An Unfinished Life*. Harper & Brothers, 1939.

Thompson, Betty Lynd. *Fundamentals of Rhythm and Dance*. Barnes, 1933.

Underhill, Evelyn. *Worship*. Harper & Brothers, 1937.

Urlin, Ethel. *Dancing, Ancient and Modern*. Appleton & Co., 1914.

Vogt, Von Ogden. *Art and Religion*. Beacon Press, 1948.

Vuillier, Gaston. *The History of Dancing*. Heinemann, London, 1898.

Warren, Florence. *The Dance of Death*. Oxford University Press, 1931.

Young, Karl. *The Drama of the Medieval Church*. Clarendon Press, 1933.